Jason Polley

To Helen, Kate and Jennifer – without whom I would smile less

Jason Polley was born in England in 1963. He has travelled to over 50 countries, spending extended periods in the Amazon, Arctic Circle, and the Sahara. Many of his adventures have been by canoe or on foot, and invariably alone. He has written many articles on survival and travel, and has advised the Royal Geographical Society on independent travel. Jason Polley still attends a great many courses on survival and outdoor pursuits to keep less frequently used skills sharp. He currently lives in the remote Scottish Highlands with his long-suffering wife, Helen, and their two daughters, Kate and Jennifer.

How to Survive Outdoors

Jason Polley

First published in Great Britain in 2013 by Hodder & Stoughton. An Hachette UK company.

First published in US in 2013 by The McGraw-Hill Companies, Inc.

Cover image © Abel Tumik/Shutterstock

Typeset by Cenveo® Publisher Services.

Printed and bound in Great Britain by CPI Group (UK) Ltd., Croydon, CRO 4YY.

Hodder & Stoughton policy is to use papers that are natural, renewable and recyclable products and made from wood grown in sustainable forests. The logging and manufacturing processes are expected to conform to the environmental regulations of the country of origin.

Hodder & Stoughton Ltd

338 Euston Road

London NW1 3BH

www.hodder.co.uk

Also available
in ebook

Acknowledgements

Illustrations by Kate Polley, Helen Polley and Jennifer Polley.

Contents

Warning

The survival techniques described in this book are for use in extreme conditions and should be performed responsibly, with caution, and with the proper regard for safety. The publishers and author cannot accept any responsibility for any prosecutions or proceedings brought or instituted against any person as a result of the use or misuse of any techniques described or any loss, injury or damage caused thereby.

Do not practise these techniques on private land without the consent of the landowner. In all cases you should check the ownership and any by-laws relating to a piece of land before you start.

How to use this book

The Teach Yourself Breakthrough series has a number of features to help you get the most out of reading this book. *How to Survive Outdoors* includes the following boxed features:

 Case studies provide a more in-depth introduction to a particular example.

 Key idea boxes distil the most important ideas and thoughts.

 Remember this boxes contain useful tips, and help you to take away what really matters.

 The **try it now** boxes contain exercises that you can start practising straightaway.

 Focus points are the key things you should remember from that chapter.

 The **next step** introduces you to the subject that follows.

Introduction

From an early age I understood that life was not about finding yourself, but about creating yourself. I wanted to create someone in myself who had more freedom, and who could survive conditions that might otherwise harm or kill. I believed that life began at the end of your comfort zone and, as much as I wanted a life full of travel and adventure, I also wanted to survive it!

To this end I set about acquiring the skills of a survivor, someone who was very comfortable outdoors and in unexpected situations. As a former Scout, I took the motto 'Be Prepared' to an extreme. Over several years, I systematically put myself through a multitude of courses. These were followed up with practice, focused reading and periodic refreshers. I learned to parachute, fly, scuba dive, climb, abseil, ride motorbikes, track, canoe, sail and shoot. I was trained in survival by SAS veteran John 'Lofty' Wiseman, and had the bushcraft expert Ray Mears teach me about tracking animals. I also did numerous medical and first aid courses, including those run by the Scottish Ambulance Service, the British Red Cross, and an excellent Wilderness Medicine course run by the Expeditionary Advisory Service of the Royal Geographical Society. I acquired a Diploma in Herbal Medicine, as I could see that this knowledge would be a huge advantage when alone in remote regions and beyond the reach of medical professionals.

During my time as a Scout I had done a basic self-defence course, and later built upon this and took classes in Shaolin Kung Fu and Ju-Jitsu.

My brothers and I would often go off hiking, sleeping rough in the Welsh mountains, or some other bleak and testing part of the country. Navigation skills soon sharpened, as did my love of living outside. I travelled abroad as often as possible, eager to experience other climates and terrains. I felt very at ease sleeping in a make-shift shelter in the Black Forest, or in a bivvy bag on a Swiss mountainside. Going to sleep in the open, staring up at the stars, or waking up to the sound of a nearby river and the dawn chorus was heaven!

I soon put my skills and knowledge to further use and travelled the globe continually, being able to go to remote places others feared, or were simply unwilling to risk hardship to reach. I spend months in the Amazon jungle, the Himalayas, the Sahara Desert, the Peruvian Andes, the Arctic Circle, and the bleaker parts of Southern Africa, Northern Europe and Central America. There was nowhere I could not get to. Timbuktu, El Dorado, Kathmandu, Outer Mongolia, China's Forbidden City, and Peru's Lost City of Machu Picchu, as well as several mountain peaks were all reached over time. My survival skills really did make a difference, as many places were challenging enough for any local people, never mind foreign travellers.

This book is, therefore, a fat-free guide to survival skills that actually work and which I have used. They kept me alive and functioning in unfamiliar and often hostile environments. You cannot always predict the future, but you can prepare for it and the possible events ahead of you. Survival skills can be your insurance if things go wrong, but also a means of extending your freedom. I always accepted that technology, team-mates and local guides would ultimately let me down. I became super self-efficient and soon was able to dispense with medical support, GPS units and kilos of supposedly essential equipment.

The more I carried in my head, the less I had to carry in my rucksack. Although Kipling was right when he said, 'He travels the fastest who travels alone', in my own experience, I found Emerson's advice just as note-worthy: 'When skating across the thin ice, our safety lies within our speed.' The speed with which you can extract yourself from a hostile environment can often dictate your chances of survival.

My interest in survival skills has only ever grown over the years. I have become fascinated with those people who refused to give up, to lie down and die. People who defied the odds, and did what others around them did not. Survivors seemed to have an attitude that enabled them to take blow after blow, set-back after set-back, and still keep going. They were able to invent and improvise, and ultimately lived. Survival could be interpreted as another word for adaptation, and this book will give several examples of people who refused to die when everyone and everything around them said throw in the towel. Stephen Hawking, the physicist, said: 'It is not clear that intelligence has any long-term survival value.' In other words, survival is not down to being more intelligent. Those who survive possess not superior intelligence, but a different way of thinking and reacting. Survivors can take more punishment, mentally and physically, and when their world changes, they change with it. And survive.

Some might say that modern life and mass urbanization has made us less able to adapt to sudden change, and that it only takes an unexpected snowfall or drought to wipe out thousands of us. Too few of us know how to navigate, to make a fire, or to filter water, but these skills are easily learned, as you will soon see. This book will not tell you about ancient Saxon shelter-making, or Inuit cooking skills. I will not bog you down with archaeological knowledge of how ancient peoples lived, or how remote tribes in the Congo survive the floods: that is for someone else in another book. This book is about teaching yourself survival skills that can be applied on your next camping trip, or put into use next time you break down in a foreign place, perhaps miles from the nearest town. It will not teach you about every edible plant found in Papua New Guinea, or how to tie 56 knots. In essence, this book aims to be practical and useful, not theoretical and simply interesting.

In our modern life it is very easy to shield yourself from nature and never experience life in a wilderness. This has resulted in many people wanting to 'get out there' and revisit a world all but lost to them. They, rightly, want to reconnect with the natural world, to reawaken an inner ancient self. Where I live in the Scottish Highlands, dozens of people die or are seriously injured each year. Many are relatively new to the remoteness of a wilderness. In most cases their death or injury is due to poor preparation, under-estimating conditions, getting lost, or simply being too casual about what life can be like once mobile phone reception ceases, and help is more than a shout away. Ignorance is killing people.

Think about what you want to be, and create yourself. Make yourself stronger, more skilled, more capable. Empower yourself, and extend your freedom and safety by teaching yourself survival skills.

This book should be treated as a course of study. The person who finishes it will be better than the one that starts it. The book is set out in several parts, and slowly builds you up and increases your knowledge and skills systematically. By the end of the book, if you also complete the practical sessions, you will be able to explore the outdoors and wilder places with greater confidence, and a much reduced risk of getting lost or injured. You will also be of more use to others.

Jason Polley
Scottish Highlands

1

Survival training

In this chapter you will learn:

▶ *What survival courses involve*
▶ *What other forms of survival training exist*
▶ *About the mental qualities of a survivor*
▶ *About the benefits of survival training*

'A fool and his well-being are soon parted'. Anyone can be uncomfortable in the outdoors, but being ill-prepared can escalate from a hardship to a fatality. Survival training offers a priceless form of insurance that can extend your freedom of movement, but also contribute to the positive outcome of an expedition or trip to unfamiliar parts.

Remember this

Survival training ought to be done well ahead of your planned trip and customized, where possible, to suit the likely conditions you expect to experience. There is no need to worry about the skills of igloo building or tickling trout if you are planning to cross a desert.

Training should be seen as involving many different forms of training materials. A course alone is not enough, any more than simply reading a book, or watching training DVDs is sufficient either. You need to immerse yourself in the subject, and get information from many different media to keep it fresh and easy to absorb.

Let's start with survival courses.

Survival courses

There is no substitute for first-hand experience and the physical practice of techniques under the guidance of an instructor. Most courses run over three or five days, with many offering basic and advanced-level training programmes.

You will be shown, and then asked to replicate, the building of shelters and fires, the collecting and purifying of water and also the identification of edible plants common to the area you are in. You often sleep in your shelter for the duration of the course. Animal traps and snares are usually constructed and you are often given little to eat other than that which you catch or collect by your own means. People get hungry.

Although people naturally cheat and bring energy bars and chocolate with them, they miss a vital lesson if they do so.

It is extremely useful to appreciate the effects of hunger and fatigue, and just how energy-sapping and difficult building a shelter under these conditions can be. You suddenly appreciate the value of saving calories, and using natural features to shelter in, rather than cutting down a dozen trees which would leave you exhausted, and little food to replace the energy spent.

Snares can often be untouched for days and edible plants are either nowhere to be seen or simply out of season. Some manuals can give the false impression that survival is simply a matter of implementing techniques, after which you'll be well fed, dry and comfortable. What is often omitted is the time and effort involved. Trying to actually catch your own food, and find edible plants, is a real lesson in what reality will be like in a real survival situation.

A majority of courses seem to be one of two types. On the one hand there are the courses run by former Special Forces personnel. These often have ex-SAS or Commandoes as instructors, and they provide a no-nonsense course, where the objective is often to survive for a shortish period until you are rescued, or get back to safety. The equipment they use is often army issue, and readily available from many army surplus suppliers. Magazines such as *Combat and Survival* cater for this group.

The other main type of course on offer is more bushcraft orientated, and attempts to make you understand and utilize the skills of ancient people who lived more with the land, or of people who still live in the wild places today. You may be taught things like how to make containers out of birch bark, treat illnesses with herbal remedies or, perhaps, carve wood into useful bowls and spoons. You learn to be at 'one with nature' far more than on a military-style course. Magazines such as *Bushcraft and Survival Skills* cater for this group.

Most will send you a kit list and programme beforehand. It would be an advantage if you had no great desire to wash or to clean your teeth for a week. Eat well before you go!

Key idea

All serious outdoors people ought to have done other courses in outdoor pursuits such as mountaineering, rock climbing, orienteering, or canoeing *in addition* to a survival course. You never can tell when one of these skills will give you the edge in an unexpected situation. Contact an established outdoor pursuit centre for details of such courses. Some are listed in Appendix 4 (Taking things further).

It must be stressed that a survival course has to be complemented with a first aid course. Follow this up with regular reviews and make yourself familiar with available treatments for common ailments such as vomiting, diarrhoea, insect bites, pain, toothache, etc.

Contact your local Red Cross Centre or your nearest Adult Education Centre for courses. Even better, volunteer to be a First Responder medic, the First Aider at work, or volunteer with one of the national organizations that provide first aid support at public events. Try to get experience of dealing with real people in real trouble. To be useful to yourself and others, you have to overcome the shock of seeing blood and real injuries.

Remember this

Medical knowledge is absolutely vital if you travel abroad or spend long periods in the wilderness.

Books

This book is to be treated as a course, or programme of study, and will encompass the key areas of outdoor survival that you need to address. However, there are more specialist survival books which cover in greater detail some aspects of survival specific to a particular region that may be relevant to you, and your type of trip.

Here are a few to take into account if you feel they would suit you:

- *RYA Sea Survival Handbook* by Keith Colwell and Steve Lucas. This is an excellent book which is designed to accompany the Royal Yacht Association's specialist sea survival course. It is an essential guide to any seaman and aimed at those to plan to undertake sea journeys on their own, or with a small crew.

- *Stay Alive in the Desert* by K E M Melville. A very useful little book by a doctor who spent many years in desert regions, and covers everything from vehicle preparation to health problems, and dealing with snakes and scorpions.

- *The Ultimate Desert Handbook* by Mark Johnson. A very detailed book which comments on all the world's desert regions and deals with the issues of water, food, medical matters, vehicle checks, as well as navigation and wildlife likely to be encountered.

- *SAS Mountain and Arctic Survival* by Barry Davies. One of the many books by ex-SAS personnel, which goes into great detail on how to survive in very cold conditions, whether they be on mountains on within the Arctic Circle.

There are, of course, a great many books to complement other skills you ought to be acquiring, such as navigation, rope work, first aid, edible plants, etc. These other books will be suggested as further reading options later on in Appendix 4 (Taking things further)

Websites

Websites such as You Tube and others have useful little clips of people demonstrating techniques such as fire starting, gutting fish, and using a compass. Use them to supplement your training, and where actual practice is proving difficult and you need to check that you have the technique right. In addition to the endless short video clips, the following sites are of great interest:

- www.equipped.org – this is the website of Equipped to Survive, a US site which states it is 'the definitive source for independent reviews and information on outdoor gear and survival equipment and techniques'. It has loads of reviews on survival kits, and good survival tips, as well as book and film reviews of all things relating to survival.

- www.bushcraft.co.uk – this is the UK-based website of Bushcraft UK, and hosts numerous articles on bushcraft and survival, in addition to book and equipment reviews, survival courses on offer, and a blog for registered members. It is a useful guide and heightens your awareness of all the survival skills you need to be acquire.

- www.survivaloutdoorskills.com – this is a website run by a former US Army Ranger and contains tips and techniques dealing with outdoor survival, and also an online shop selling books and survival equipment.

DVDs

There are not too many purely instructional films or programmes readily available, other than slightly amateur ones available directly from specialist magazines. Consequently, if you are desperate to see something done and can't get on a course, find a clip on the Internet. As more of an entertainment and overview I would suggest watching some of the many TV programmes by both Ray Mears and Bear Grylls.

From the point of view of learning survival skills, Ray Mears' TV series *Extreme Survival* is pretty good, as is his *Bushcraft* series. Being a former SAS man, Bear Grylls is quite different and deals more with getting out of a hostile place you have found yourself in by accident. His *Born Survivor* TV series will help you think like a survivor, and appreciate the power of the 'who dares wins' principle.

Fitness

Key idea

In addition to acquiring actual skills and knowledge, a person with above average fitness has an above average chance of survival. Keep yourself fit, join a gym and do two to three all-body workouts a week. When things go wrong, the fitter and stronger you are, the easier it usually is to cope and pull through.

Become a regular runner and swimmer, and hike whenever you can. Improve your health, fitness and strength and it will cut you some slack when you have to go to Plan B and walk an unexpected distance, perhaps carrying a friend, or with an injury.

Case study

In August 1944, during the Second World War, the American submarine USS *Flier* struck a mine in the Sulu Sea, and soon began to sink. Of the 80-man crew, only eight managed to survive. The submarine went down, but the eight surviving crew members stayed alive by swimming for some *17 hours* until they reached an uninhabited island. Their fantastic level of fitness and their swimming skills saved their lives. Although they still had to evade the enemy and get back to safety, they are a testament to the supreme advantage of being fit.

Their story is told in full in *Eight Survived* by Douglas A Campbell.

Practice

Remember this

Knowledge becomes rusty if unused and techniques soon become forgotten. You must physically practise what you have learned; you must regularly refresh your memory by re-reading the survival tips and strategies in this book.

Regular practice is vital, and key practical skills must be put to use in order for you to be able to rely on them at a later date. Would you have much faith in a surgeon that passed his medical course several years ago, but then did no further training, refresher courses or hands-on practice until needing to operate on you?

Get into the habit of carrying a compass with you and practise identifying north by natural means, checking yourself against the compass. Go camping/hiking as frequently as you can. Spend time in a make-shift shelter, cook a meal over an open fire, and see if you can light it without a match. Do this in comfortable conditions, perhaps over the summer. Once you think you have mastered a technique, such as fire starting or shelter building, repeat the task in the rain or over the winter period. Try to replicate what a real survival situation might demand of you.

You must keep putting into practice these simple but often life-saving techniques. You have to be comfortable and at ease in what might be called a disaster or 'survival situation'.

Try it now

Get out in all seasons and experience what it is like to navigate in the rain, or build a fire in a snow storm. As they say: train hard, fight easy. The better your preparations, the easier it will be to deal with set-backs and the unexpected.

We have all seen television documentaries of rescue and survival. I hope none of us are ever the subject of such programmes as the common denominator in many cases is sheer foolhardiness and a total disregard for planning and preparation. Learn from others' mistakes.

Mental attitude

Research into human survival has been conducted, specifically looking at survivors of air and sea disasters. One of the deciding factors in whether you survive or not is generally believed to be the personality of the individual.

Introverts invariably died in their seats, as they simply sat waiting for someone to tell them what to do. Extroverts however, waited for no such instructions and climbed out to safety as soon as they could, often over those introverts frozen to their seats. Clear, assertive action can save your life.

If disaster does strike, be proactive in getting out, and do not wait for a leader to tell you what to do. Be the leader. Help others where you can, but do not wait to be told where to go or what action to take.

Another important factor research has identified is training and personal experience. Those who have experience of something similar (either in real life or on a training course) are less likely to be paralysed by shock and die through non-action. The shock of the disaster can inhibit clear thinking and decisive action. By being less easy to shock, you are more able to think and act to your advantage. Whereas most of us are familiar with the fight or flight options when confronted with something life threatening, the lethal third option of paralysis and being frozen to the spot, should also be taken into account. Acknowledge it, and break from it if you find yourself doing nothing.

I have heard survival experts say that the overriding factor in determining who lives and who dies is the individuals' state of mind. The right mental attitude, that never-say-die mentality, seems far more important that being able to navigate by the stars or ignite twigs in the rain.

Psychologists tell us if we concentrate and visualize a positive outcome to a situation it is more likely to become a reality than if we don't. Negativity breeds failure. If you allow the situation to get on top of you, you will find it very difficult to draw upon energy reserves, and so will be very tempted to just lie down and let fate (and often death) take over.

Remember this

Survival training needs to go beyond the learning of a few useful techniques. It needs to indelibly impress upon you the fact that death is not an option. Although you'll probably need a shower and a clean shirt at the end of it, the situation will not kill you. Lack of food and water are an inconvenience but you *will* pull through.

Common qualities to most survivors are an ability to:

▶ think clearly and not panic

▶ have a positive, optimistic attitude

▶ 'tune in' to new situations and not be shocked easily

- hold pain and discomfort in check
- see the bigger picture and not fret over trivia
- be assertive and decisive
- lead the way, and not be overly reliant on others

Survival is usually dependent on having the right kit, the right training and the right mental attitude. Take your life and safety seriously, if for no other reason than others may depend on you.

Focus points

* Survival training includes learning survival techniques, but also other skills such as mountaineering, canoeing, navigation and first aid.
* Survival courses are only part of survival training, and books, websites, DVDs and regular practice sessions on your own are all part of equipping yourself.
* Physical fitness can give you a real edge when things go wrong.
* Survivors think differently and act differently, and knowledge of survival techniques are not always as important as having the right frame of mind.

Next step

Having got to grips with what survival training is all about, you need to move on to learning about some useful items of equipment to carry with you and to building your own survival kit. Having the correct equipment and kit can make a difference between life and death in an extreme situation where your life is truly hanging in the balance.

2

Survival kits and equipment

In this chapter you will learn:

- ▶ *The role of a survival kit*
- ▶ *The key components of a kit*
- ▶ *About other useful equipment*
- ▶ *Where to carry survival equipment*

Get into the habit of being able to improvise, to make do, to create and invent, and use your survival kit to supplement your knowledge and resourcefulness. For example, if you lose your compass, know how to navigate by other means; if you don't have a water filter know how to make an improvised one. Do not overplay the value of equipment; it is useful, but your survival need not depend on it.

The basic survival kit

Here is a list of useful items to consider including, but they are only a starting point as to what your kit could contain:

Flint and striker: Produces thousands of sparks by scraping a piece of flint against a piece of steel. Some variants have a piece of magnesium, which you shave pieces off into a small pile, then ignite with the striker. It will burn well and hopefully ignite your kindling and twigs. It is a good idea to practise lighting a fire with a spark before you actually need to. Cotton wool is particularly easy to ignite with just a spark. These flint strikers are very handy little things, last for ages, and work even if they get wet. (See Figure 2.1.)

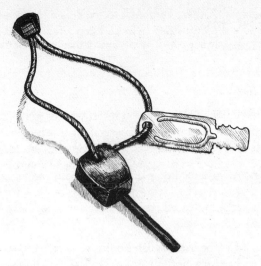

Figure 2.1 Striker (© Kate Polley)

Matches: Either buy specially made survival matches, or dip non-safety ones in molten wax to waterproof them. Store them in a waterproof container within a survival kit, or within a pocket of a jacket you wear on outdoor trips. Red-tipped non-safety matches can work even after getting wet and being dried out; brown-tipped safety matches do not work at all once they get wet.

Fishing kit: Include a selection of hooks, weights, flies and a length of fishing line. You can use the items to catch birds and game, as well as fish. However, it is not necessarily worth including if your trip is to a desert area, but does depend where an accident or Plan B route might take you. Practise using it and assembling it before you actually need it. Make a rod from a stick, tie some line and hooks, and see what it is like to fish with.

Water purification tablets: I find iodine-based ones the best. Always follow the manufacturers' directions and make sure you use them within the shelf life. Filter the water as best you can *before* using the tablets. Water purification tablets work better on water that does not have visible bits of debris floating about (read the next chapter on water) and even make-shift water filters will help. Drinking poor-quality water could make your situation a whole lot worse.

Small compass: A spare compass, like spares of other useful kit, is a must (see the case study below). Keep a few dotted about your kit and clothing.

 Try it now

Sew a small button compass into your usual jacket, as well as keeping one in your survival kit.

Painkillers: Always include painkillers as pain can impair clear thinking and lead to accidents and mistakes. Check use-by dates, and only give to others if you are sure they have no allergies to aspirin, etc.

Safety pins: Can be used as fish hooks, to hold bandages in place, to secure torn clothing, etc. They are useful items that can make an unplanned struggle just a bit more bearable.

Candles: Carry a few 'magic' birthday candles that relight after you have blown them out. They are ideal in windy conditions and save on matches. This is the first thing to light once your fire is ready to be lit. If the match blows out, you need not waste another match trying to get your fire going, as the magic candle will keep relighting, and hopefully get your fire alight, even in windy conditions.

Wire saw: For cutting through larger branches when making rafts, shelters, traps, etc. They can go rusty, so smear with grease and check regularly to see if they need replacing. Practise using one, as if used too vigorously it will snap. Try to carry more than one. They are quite energy-consuming, so don't rush to use one unless you have to.

Scalpel blades: Good for skinning and cutting fish and game. They are easier to use if you make or take a handle. Carry two or three of differing shapes. Craft shops often have them for sale, but otherwise try a chemist.

Brass wire: Ideal for making snares and animal traps. Picture-framing wire is a common source; coil up a metre or more for general use.

Heliograph or mirror: For signalling purposes. These are more suited to sunny conditions where you have plenty of wide open spaces, such as a desert, and are not always that necessary on trips to the jungle or in mountain areas where low cloud is frequent. If you have space, pack one.

Potassium permanganate: Any good chemist will sell this. It can be used to sterilize water by adding enough to turn the water bright pink. Add more to turn the water deep pink and use as a disinfectant. In large quantities it will stain snow a purple colour for attracting rescuers. I like kit to be as multi-functional as possible, and this stuff is just that.

Needle and thread: Primarily used to repair clothing and kit. Ensure that the needle has a large eye so that you can use heavy thread to sew up damaged rucksacks, jackets, etc. Pack some strong nylon thread, so it could be used for snares or heavy repairs if need be.

Condom: Can hold about two pints of water if poured in, but carry carefully as they will burst. Can also be used as a catapult, elastic, or as a binding. As they are sterile, they can be put over the ends of fingers and used in medical situations.

I would suggest putting the items in something like a fairly large metal tin, then packing the spare spaces with cotton wool to stop anything rattling about. Cotton wool can also be used for fire-lighting as it will ignite with a spark very easily. The tin itself can be used to boil up small quantities of water and the lid can be shined to use as a heliograph. Seal the tin with duct tape. If a tin is not appropriate, use a plastic food box. The survival kit should be as waterproof as you can make it.

Case study

For a while I worked within the Arctic Circle as a guide, mostly taking people to the remoter parts of northern Scandinavia. We were helicoptered in, and after unloading and inflating a large Avon rubber raft, would return to civilization a few weeks later by following the rivers downstream, bouncing through the rapids along the way. Many in the group were keen bird watchers, or just fancied an adventurous few weeks.

On one such trip, there were just three paying customers and myself. We had a good-quality map, Silva compass and enough food for the duration of the journey back, about ten days as I recall. Within hours of being dropped off, and the helicopter being out of sight, we realized there was going to be a problem. Several sections of the river were too low to float our raft. After several hours of running and scouting ahead, the situation did not appear to improve. The information I had been given about water levels and rainfalls had been wrong. We had no radio, and mobile phones were not widely available at that time. We were on our own, and as the guide, I had to do something about it. It was unlikely we would be able to get to our pick-up point, or near a town, within the time we had planned or before the food ran out.

I had to come up with a Plan B. I checked the map and decided we would have to carry the raft and kit to another river several miles away. By taking a different route altogether, we should be able to get back to our rendezvous point in time for the scheduled pick-up. Somehow, during this very long and difficult trek, our Silva compass was lost. We were in a vast people-less wilderness, with no means of communication, and with limited food. If we took the wrong tributary in the raft, we could easily become lost, take more time, and food would run out.

Fortunately, I had a small button compass sewn into my jacket, a jacket I hardly ever took off. This small but accurate compass kept us on the right bearing, and steered us safely home within our allotted time, and before food ran out.

To lose a compass can be dangerous, and this should not have happened. We were tired, irritated and stressed. Our vigilance dropped because we had to carry the raft and our kit for hours on end over difficult, boggy terrain, with mosquitoes biting us all the time. Accidents happen. I should have been more careful, but this is how life or death situations sneak up on you. However, having a back-up compass made all the difference, and forward planning, done months before, paid off.

OTHER ITEMS OF KIT TO CONSIDER

In my experience the two most useful items in a survival situation, that are also quite difficult to improvise, are a strong sharp knife and a cooking pot.

► Knives

Remember this

You need something strong and heavy that can cut and chop through thick wood to help make a raft or a shelter, serve as a hunting spear, or clear jungle paths, etc. Your scalpel blades won't do, nor will the blade of a penknife or multi-tool. Axes, machetes or parangs are ideal.

Some types of knife contain a survival kit in the hollow handle. My concern with this is, if you lose your knife, you lose your kit.

The knife has to be strong and solid to be of any use, and therefore will usually be heavy and quite large. These very features make such knives a problem to carry on you at all times, particularly if you have to travel through populated areas during your trip. Having a large Tarzan-style knife swinging from your belt draws unwanted attention. Also, as most rucksacks have a waist belt nowadays, doing the belt up over a sheath knife is uncomfortable and likely to create a sore where the knife presses into you. In practice, the heavy knife or small axe tends to get put in the rucksack. If the rucksack is lost, or has to be ditched for some reason, (e.g. a river crossing, to escape a dangerous animal, etc.) you lose your knife. If the knife is contained your survival kit, you lose that too. If you want to carry a survival knife with a small kit in the handle, make sure you *never* take it off and carry it *on* you at all times.

Try it now

In addition to a larger knife and a selection of scalpel blades, get into the habit of carrying a Gerber or Leatherman-type multi tool in your trouser pocket, or on your belt at all times. Knives are only useful if kept sharp, so carry a means of sharpening them. There are many small portable knife sharpeners available; buy one or two and always have one with you. A blunt knife can be dangerous and also useless.

Do not associate your ability to survive with large, scary knives. Knives may help your survival, but sharp stones and bits of glass or metal can often be found to cut what needs cutting.

▶ Cooking pot

Military style mess tins are ideal as they can also act as storage for high-calorie food. Where space is more limited, I carry a metal 500 ml (one-pint) mug also stuffed with high-calorie food. Boiling water is very difficult without a metal container of some sort and survival food is best served as a stew or soup to ensure that nothing nutritious is lost.

If you are going to carry a large mug or mess tins in a pouch on your belt, you could then use it to house your survival kit. Pack spare spaces with high-calorie foods.

▶ Other useful kit

Basic medical kit: In addition to the usual bandages and plasters, carry medicines to treat diarrhoea, stomach upsets, pain, cuts and toothache. Any chemist will assist. Your doctor may be willing to give you antibiotics and other prescription medicines. Make up your own kit, rather than buy a pre-packed one. (See the next chapter on first aid and medicine to get a better idea of what medicines to carry.)

Basha: Having a means of shelter can be very useful and time saving. Ponchos, bashas, bivvy bags or even a sheet of plastic will do. Carry what space allows. I used to regularly go camping with a friend who could construct a waterproof tent from six black bin bags. They folded down to nothing, and could often be used to supplement the shelter he was making from a fallen tree or lean-to against a rock wall.

Paracord: The inner cords can be pulled out and used as fishing line or for jobs where thinner line is more appropriate. This cord is very strong and very useful. Many people re-lace their boots with it, and then melt the ends to prevent fraying. It is always worth carrying a couple of metres if you can.

Wristwatch with a second hand: Useful for psychological reasons, as knowing the time and date gives some structure to an otherwise chaotic situation. Useful for checking a pulse in medical situations, and also when using water purification tablets as some require the water being left for a prescribed amount of time before the water is safe to drink.

Watches can also be used for navigation purposes and also for estimating distances covered, as we walk at about four miles per hour. Suunto, Casio and Timex all produce watches with in-built digital compasses, barometers and altimeters. They make a very useful back-up compass if nothing else.

Thermal underwear: A set of Helly Hansen long johns and top, or something similar, are invaluable. This stuff screws up into nothing and can easily be carried in a jacket pocket. It will keep you warm and add a vital layer. It also has superb wicking properties which means if you start to sweat the moisture is drawn away from your skin so you don't freeze when you cool down. It can make life a little warmer when cold starts to slow you down and impair your judgement.

Boots: Take your footwear seriously and get a good tough pair of boots. I prefer leather as they are cooler in the heat, warmer in the cold, tough, and are largely waterproof. Look after them and treat them regularly with dubbin, Nikwax, or any other waterproofing treatment. Your boots are like the wheels on a car: neglect them and you'll go nowhere.

Food: Space permitting, carry high-calorie food that will see you through a period when food is in short supply. I favour dried fruit and nuts as they keep for ages and don't melt. If it is wrapped up well, always carry chocolate as well. Remember to only eat if water is available, as water is needed for digestion, and dehydration will worsen if you eat while under-hydrated.

Torch: A Maglite or one with multiple LED lights is ideal but ensure that it is waterproof and robust. Frequently check the battery life and that they are not leaking. Torches are never that vital, but can make signalling and doing things in the dark much easier. If space is tight, leave it out.

Credit card tool: There are now several credit card-sized tools on the market. Some, although only millimetres thick, have torches, knives, compasses, scissors and tweezers assembled in a wafer-thin card. They can easily be slipped into your wallet and serve as a useful backup in unexpected situations.

Clothing: I know it sounds obvious, but wear appropriate clothing. Layer your clothes and adjust as the temperature changes. Jackets with hoods will keep you warmer and dryer than those without. Light-weight trousers will dry out quicker than denim jeans. A pair of leather gloves will enable you to handle hot or sharp items plus protect you from the cold. Scarves will help keep you warm and could double up as a bandage.

Key idea

Survival is largely about anticipating and preparing. Any equipment must be as multi-functional as possible, and essential survival items should always be *on you*, not in the car, not in your rucksack. This means having a survival kit in a small pouch on your belt all the times, or at least having some key survival items in the pockets of your trousers or jacket. If you have to abandon a rucksack for some reason, you need to be left with some kit still on you.

Travel documents and money should be protected from water and sweat, and kept securely either within a length of tubigrip around your leg or in a secure pouch somewhere *on your body*. Again, do not keep them in a vehicle or in a bag.

▶ Useful suppliers

Check the classifieds of the various outdoor magazines mentioned in Appendix 4 (Taking things further), for local suppliers, but ready-made survival kits, credit card-size tools, ponchos, paracord, etc. can be obtained from one of the outdoor equipment suppliers mentioned.

Focus points

* Survival kits are aids to survival, and should not be viewed as vital to it. Do not depend on a piece of equipment so heavily that without it you risk your safety.
* Survival kits and equipment should be customized to your likely circumstances.
* All kit and equipment should be reviewed and checked to ensure nothing deteriorates and it all stays useful.
* Equipment should be as multi-functional as possible.
* Vital equipment, such as your survival kit, should be on you at all times.

Next step

Now you are getting into the right frame of mind and equipping yourself with the right kit, you need to acquire the skills and knowledge to deal with the survival basics: food and water, fire and shelter, signalling and navigation.

3

Water

In this chapter you will learn:

- ► *The importance of water*
- ► *How to detect and prevent dehydration*
- ► *How to find water*
- ► *How to make water safe to drink*

Water must always be uppermost in your mind when on any hike, expedition or venture into the outdoors. All forms of life quickly deteriorate and die without it. Although dehydration can kill in its own right, it is usually the effects of dehydration, including mental confusion and irritability, which invariably lead to bad decisions and accidents, both of which could be life threatening.

Remember this

When planning any trip outdoors, consider what opportunities there will be to refill your water. Carry what you can, but identify areas where you can replenish your water bottles and containers.

Even in our mild British climate, you still need at least 2–3 litres per day, and considerably more if physically exerting yourself. Even mild dehydration can significantly impair your physical and mental performance.

The typical early warning symptoms of dehydration include:

▶ dark urine

▶ headaches

▶ irritability

▶ fatigue

▶ nausea

▶ ringing in your ears

The condition worsens to delirium, slurred speech, dizziness, and ultimately death. It is often unnoticed until quite advanced, so you must drink periodically regardless of how thirsty you feel. Thirst is a poor indicator of your water requirements, more so in cold or humid conditions. It is often better to work in pairs if you are in a team so that you can look out for each other, as dehydration is one of those conditions that is not always detected by the sufferer.

Water retention

If water is in limited supply, take immediate action to reduce dehydration:

► Eat less, especially fatty foods, as water is needed in the digestion process.

► Do not smoke, and refrain from drinking coffee or alcohol.

► Stop talking and only breathe through your nose. Water, as vapour, is lost every time you open your mouth.

► Minimize your discomfort by sucking pebbles or a button to keep the mouth and throat moist.

► Keep cool by wetting clothes in undrinkable water, e.g. sea-water, even urine.

► Avoid physical activity during the hottest parts of the day.

► Wear loose clothing and cover exposed skin to reduce water loss through evaporation.

► Get out of the sun and heat if you can, and do not lie or sit on any hot surfaces.

Case study

The enormous importance of water was made all too clear in the 1994 desert ultra marathon, the infamous Marathon des Sables in the Moroccan Sahara. This seven-day event has runners attempting a 145-mile route through the sandy desert in unbearable heat and conditions, being responsible for their supplies and equipment.

One entrant was a 39-year-old Italian policeman, Mauro Prosperi. He had been caught in a sandstorm and had lost his way. Prosperi realized he had been separated from all the other entrants, and the route had become totally obscured by the storm and had melted into the desert. Unsure where to go, he ran on regardless, not realizing he was going in the wrong direction altogether.

Within a few days, his supplies had run out and his water all gone. He found an abandoned mosque and took temporary shelter. Severely dehydrated, he managed to catch two bats, broke their necks and drank as much blood out of them as he could, in an attempt to get some liquids into him. He later caught a snake, and even resorted to drinking his urine. At his lowest point, he scratched a farewell message on a wall, and tried to slit his wrists with a penknife. However, his dehydrated state was so extreme, that his blood had thickened too much to flow out, and he failed to take his own life.

For whatever reason or logic, Prosperi then decided to leave the mosque and headed back out into the unforgiving desert. This act of virtual insanity saved him, as he came upon some nomads who provided immediate care and water, and brought him safely back to the race's organizers.

Prosperi lived through his ordeal by drinking liquids from animals most would not consider. This bought him valuable time, and enabled him to stay alive just long enough to be rescued.

Finding water

As the Chinese proverb goes, 'A wise man digs a well before he is thirsty'. *Before* you become too physically weak or delirious, you must find adequate water.

It must be stressed that you have to use several water-gathering methods simultaneously to ensure enough water is obtained. Do not rely on one method alone. In the absence of any obvious rivers or lakes, you must look for signs indicating the presence of water. These include:

▶ Bees, ants, and flies – all of which are never far from water.

▶ Grain and grass-feeding birds and mammals. Follow their tracks up hill and see if you can find their source. Note: meat eaters are poor indicators of water as they derive liquid from the blood they consume.

- ► Clumps of grass are often indicators of wetter, perhaps boggy ground.

- ► Mixed vegetation of several different plants, again would suggest underlying water.

Additionally, note the lie of the land and try digging at the outside bend of dry riverbeds, or valley bottoms where water looks like it would drain naturally. Have regard to your own sweating in trying to dig for water, as you do not want to worsen your condition and accelerate the effects of dehydration. Work slowly and steadily, preferably in the cooler part of the day.

Remember this

If collecting water from a river, always try to draw water from the middle, as water runs fastest – and therefore cleanest – in the centre. Be cautious of still water, especially if it is devoid of green plants and smells foul: the water may be contaminated. I saw whole lakes near villages in Central America cordoned off as being cholera infected. The cholera bacterium can live naturally in any environment, but is usually associated with poor sanitation. Water sources near villages and settlements in developing countries should therefore be treated with the utmost caution.

Be alert to chemical contamination of water sources. Proper disposal practices are not always adhered to, and farmers and factories are sometimes responsible for the contamination of land and water sources. If you see other birds and animals drinking from the source, or perhaps can see numerous tracks indicating this to be their water source, it might be safe enough to collect. However, if there are few bank-side plants, the water looks or smells odd, and there are no animal signs on the muddy bank, it is probably safer to leave it.

Collect rain water where you can, even by allowing clothing to soak it up, and wringing it out later before it starts to dry. Wet grass and soil can be blotted with absorbent cloth and also wrung out into a container.

Along coastal areas, dig a well at least a hundred metres from the high tide mark. The water may be brackish, but drinkable. If need be you can distil saltwater by boiling it up and covering the pot with a cloth to catch the steam. By regularly wringing out the cloth you will be collecting salt-free water.

In snowy areas avoid eating snow as it aids dehydration. Instead, squeeze it into tight snowballs and suck it.

Key idea

Collecting water is slow and tiring, often resulting in tiny amounts of liquid being gathered. You therefore have to start looking for water before dehydration takes effect, and to collect water by as many means as possible.

WATER FROM PLANTS

A plant's roots draw water up from the ground and distribute it around the whole plant. Fortunately for you, this valuable liquid can be teased out by condensation.

Try it now

Cover a leafy part of the plant with a (preferably black) plastic bag. Seal the bag by tying it on tightly or using some duct tape, and leave for a while. Drinkable water will collect through condensation inside the bag. Carefully remove the bag, and drink the liquid. The bigger the bag, and the greater the number of bags used, the larger the amount of water collected.

Some plants such as barrel cacti and coconuts are rich in drinkable liquids, but avoid white, milky sap as a rule. Jungle vines can be cut and the dripping liquid collected and drunk immediately. Shake thicker bamboo stems and listen for trapped water inside. Bore a small hole in each section to extract the water.

Obviously fruit and vegetables are rich in water and should be eaten if discovered. Be cautious of eating too much, particularly if unripe, as it may produce diarrhoea, which leads back to dehydration.

SOLAR STILL

This well-known device (see 'Try it now' below) can be used to collect water more or less anywhere but is more effective if a clear plastic sheet is used of about 2–3 square metres. As with the plant bags described above, the more you use, the more water you gather. Do not rely upon this method as your sole source of water; it only produces a little and takes quite a while to do even that. However, it is one of those methods that can be put in place while you go off and look for water elsewhere. See Figure 3.1 overleaf.

Try it now

Dig a hole around 30 cm deep and about a metre across. Put your water container in the bottom. Spread the plastic sheet across the top of the hole, and put a stone or weight in the middle so that the dip hangs just above your container. Weigh the edges of the sheet down with stones and earth and try to make it as airtight as possible.

Water will collect on the underside of the plastic sheet and drip into your container. To increase production, you can put urine or vegetation into the hole before sealing it up.

It is easier to run a thin tube from your container to the surface to save you digging it all up to get to the water.

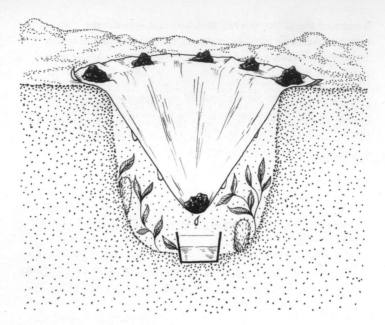

Figure 3.1 Solar still (© Kate Polley)

WATER FILTRATION

This need only be done when water is gathered from rivers or bodies of water. You do not need to filter water gathered from solar stills, plants or snow.

Good preparation will help here. There are numerous very portable filtration kits on the market now. Filtration straws can be used to drink straight from a water source. Get some and carry them at all times. Your life could depend on it.

Purification tablets are easy to carry and use. Purification tablets work more effectively if added to relatively clear water. Allow muddy water to settle and then draw off the top section into another container. Iodine is preferred as it can kill off most of the nastier bugs found worldwide. Always carry some and follow the instructions. Be aware that some tablets need to be left for a set time before their active ingredients have worked and made the water safe to drink.

If none of the above is available, you can still clean the water with a make-shift filter. Either put one sock inside the other, or use a pair of trousers and put one trouser leg inside the other and tie off the bottom to make a tubular sack. Put lumps of cold charcoal (NOT ash) into the bottom. Alternatively, or as well, add fine sand. Pour the dirty water through your filter a few times. Afterwards, boil for at least five minutes. This is not 100 per cent guaranteed to kill or remove all the nasties, but it will make a difference.

INDIAN WELL

If you cannot find a stream or any deep water to collect, but the ground feels wet and saturated, you may be able to use an Indian Well to extract water from the soil. Find a dip or low point in the ground and dig a hole half a metre deep and half a metre wide. Initially, the water that seeps in will be dirty (which you could still filter and use), but if you carefully scoop out the water, it gradually becomes cleaner. Eventually you will have clear(ish) water. I would still suggest boiling it before drinking.

ANIMAL SOURCES

Many native people drink blood as a nutrient, as well as a means of hydration, particularly in desert and savannah regions. Cattle herders in some developing countries regularly nick the necks of their cows to draw out some blood to drink. Eye balls contain a safe liquid too, and the eyes of fish have been frequently sucked out as a means of survival by those shipwrecked or stranded in drifting life rafts. If you are dehydrating, do not only think of water, think of all safe liquids, be they from plants, the ground or animals.

Rehydration

It is important that you do not gulp down water if you need to rehydrate yourself. This will induce vomiting and further dehydration. Instead, take regular small sips. Water absorption and your well-being are improved if you add a pinch of salt and two teaspoons of sugar to each cup you drink. Check the colour of your urine to see if you have taken in enough liquids – the paler it is, the more hydrated you are. Slowly rehydrate yourself, and your recovery will be more comfortable, and you will feel better almost instantly.

Focus points

✳ When venturing outdoors, always plan ahead so water bottles and containers can be refilled at some known point.

✳ Look out for signs of dehydration in yourself and those with you.

✳ Slow down dehydration where possible and conserve body fluid.

✳ Animals, birds and insects are good indicators of a nearby water source.

✳ Valuable water can be extracted from plants and the earth.

✳ Water should be filtered and purified before drinking.

Next step

Another of the key skills required by a survivor in the outdoors is the ability to make and start a fire. This is often required under difficult and perhaps wet conditions, which is when survival situations often unfold. The uses of fire go beyond just keeping you warm, and can enhance your chances of survival considerably.

4

Fire

In this chapter you will learn:

▶ *About the uses of fire*
▶ *How to construct a fire*
▶ *The means of igniting a fire*
▶ *How to light a fire in wet conditions*

Fire, although not always necessary for survival, is extremely useful for several reasons. A great many situations can be improved by having a fire, and a survivor needs to understand these benefits and be able to make a fire in a variety of conditions.

Fire can be used to:

▶ boil and purify water that would be harmful untreated

▶ cook food that might be toxic or foul otherwise

▶ provide warmth, and perhaps ward off hypothermia

▶ dry out wet clothing and boots

▶ signal for help

▶ protect from unwanted animals and insects

▶ raise morale

Fire preparation

Choose a suitably sheltered site for your fire. Clear the ground and surrounding area of anything that could burn unintentionally, such as dry leaves and grass. Also, either dig a shallow pit or build a low wall around your fire site with stones or large sticks. This both stops the fire spreading uncontrollably and prevents the wind blowing it out or fanning it unnecessarily.

Remember this

Collect all the combustible material you need *before* trying to start the fire. I have seen too many people get their tinder and kindling alight only to watch it burn out as they rush around trying to find more wood. Collect all the required wood and materials before thinking about trying to light anything.

Firstly, you will need **tinder** – very thin sticks, sawdust, paper, cloth, strips of silver birch bark, cotton wool, dry grass, bark, etc. This material has to be very dry and is vital as it is the stuff your initial spark, or match, ignites. I find it best to collect tinder throughout the day as I see it, and then store it in a pocket until needed. This keeps it dry, which is what may be hardest to find when it comes to making a fire.

If you cannot easily find suitable tinder, make your own by using a sharp knife to produce a large handful of paper-thin shavings – imagine you are sharpening a pencil. These will burn very easily and produce heat to ignite the other materials.

Next, you need **kindling** – slightly larger sticks, about the thickness of a pencil, perhaps split in half to make them easier to burn. Again, make sure that you have plenty before lighting the fire. Lastly, have the larger materials to hand: anything from finger-thick sticks to large branches.

Have all your wood or other material set out in bundles ready to go on. Do not ignite the tinder, then scramble about trying to find something for it to burn. You do not want to risk your tinder or kindling going out through lack of wood. No match or spark must be wasted.

Remember this

Once you have the fire going, blow gently at the base of it if it starts to die down prematurely. This should provide enough oxygen to raise the temperature in order to ignite the unburnt material. Keep fanning or blowing the base, gently at first, to ensure the fire heats up and starts burning the wood.

Fire starting

Your tinder can be set alight by one of the following methods:

▶ Matches: carry specially prepared waterproof survival matches, which also burn a lot longer too.

▶ Lighter: liquid fuel types dry out quickly and gas ones can leak. You may be left with nothing but a spark to use.

▶ Steel/flint sparkers: these produce thousands of fire-lighting sparks even when wet.

Try it now

Practise igniting various types of tinder with a sparker. Play around with various types of tinder, and get to know how to feather up a strip of silver birch bark so it lights with only a spark.

▶ Magnifying glass: useful in sunny conditions with very dry tinder. Camera lenses, glass bottles and binoculars have also been used to focus the sun's heat to start a fire.

▶ Electrical batteries: connect a wire to each terminal then touch the ends among a piece of wire wool or your tinder. You'll need more than an AA battery however. Small 9V batteries or larger car batteries usually work well.

▶ Friction: this works, but you do need the right materials and proper technique (see 'Try it now' below). Perfect the skill before you actually need it; a real survival situation is not the place to try out a technique you have never practised before. In essence, it works by rubbing dry wood against wood with such speed and friction that embers are produced that you can then ignite your tinder with. You need a bow a drill, and a base.

Try it now

Make yourself a 1 metre bow, and tie a strong cord between the two ends. Cut a straight 30 cm stick ('the drill') and shape the ends to blunt cones. You then need a flat wood base with a small hollow dip cut out near the edge, about 1 cm across. Cut a V-shaped notch from the outside edge to the dip to collect the (hopefully) burning embers you are going to produce. Now place the drill in the dip, thread the bow's cord around it and work the bow so that the drill spins as you pull it back and forth (see Figure 4.1). It helps if you press down on the drill by placing a block of hard wood on top to steady the action and to maintain a downward pressure.

As the temperature in the hollow dip rises, smoke will start to be produced and charcoal dust will collect. Blow lightly to keep it ignited and then transfer to your tinder. Experiment with this method and try it out long before you need to rely on it. I have seen people start fires this way with comparative ease, but it does take practice. If you have no other means of starting a fire, it is worth trying.

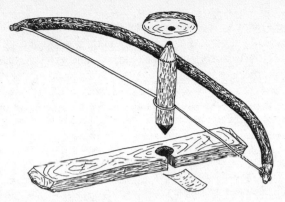

Figure 4.1 Fire drill (© Kate Polley)

You can also ignite your tinder with various chemicals, firearms, flares and explosives. However, these items are rarely to hand in a survival situation for most of us, and I would suggest you learn how to ignite tinder with the main methods above so that the loss of your usual matches or lighter does not mean you cannot start a fire.

Remember this

Practise fire starting under different conditions, using different materials. Become an expert so that fire making is something you can do without hesitation or any trouble. It is one of the key basic skills and something you must become very proficient at.

Case study

While on a canoe expedition in a remote part of northern Sweden, it started to rain heavily. Although we changed into waterproofs, we were all very wet, and cold, within minutes. Our intended stopping point for the day was still several hours away, and the tundra-like landscape offered no trees as temporary cover from the persistent rain. We paddled on miserably.

After a few hours of slow progress and body temperatures beginning to drop dangerously, we came upon a small clump of twisted birch trees. As the group's leader, I made a decision to pull in and try to make a fire from the few trees ahead to warm everyone up.

I cleared a metre by metre area on the ground and made a platform from sticks. The fire would ultimately sit on these sticks and not directly on the wet boggy ground. I then collected as much wood as I could from the birch trees. I split open the branches to expose the dry insides, and cut away the very wet outer layers. I set all the wood out in neat batches under a tent fly sheet, which I had quickly put up for this very purpose.

I cut the birch bark into thin sheets and strips and wrapped them in pieces of tissue paper which we had with us. This would be the tinder, and I made lots of it. For the kindling, I split open quite large branches, and cut out sections of the dry wood deep within. I shaved them into thin sticks, and made sure I had plenty of them. Once alight, they would provide the essential heat to dry out and ignite the larger-sized pieces of wood I would be putting on top. This next grade of wood was finger- and arm-thick branches, which again I split open to expose the drier interiors.

I initially started the fire under the protection of a fly sheet from another of our tents. However, once the tinder and kindling caught, I removed this as the fire was strong enough not to be put out by the rain, and I could not risk damaging the tent's fly sheet. Once the tinder caught alight, I knelt down, and stayed very close to the base of the fire, gently blowing it and providing additional oxygen to the weak fire. The fire was very smoky to start with as the wood was still quite damp. As the fire grew, I still kept blowing and fanning it, steadily putting on more wood.

Eventually the fire was roaring, and the rain fortunately lessened. The cold, wet group gathered round to dry off and warm up. Water was put on to boil, and hot drinks and packet soups were hastily consumed. Core temperatures, and morale, rose.

Being able to make a fire in this case, prevented the risk of hypothermia, which is a constant worry when doing outdoor activities in cold, wet conditions. The fire enabled us to make hot drinks to dry out some clothes, and it raised much needed morale.

Remember this

Strips of birch bark burn very easily even when damp, and make excellent tinder and kindling. Collect some whenever you see it, for later use. Any cotton wool, or cotton wool type material, can be ignited by spark alone, so it is useful to carry some. You can also use bits of medical dressings if you have some and are desperate.

I also find it very useful to carry a block or so of solid fuel such as hexamine or Zip fire-lighters. They are easy to burn and make life easier when things go belly up. Carry a block or two in a waterproof bag with your tinder.

'Magic' birthday candles that re-ignite after being blown out are a godsend. They save matches and effort and are ideal for carrying in a survival tin. I sometimes carry a fire kit in a small tobacco tin separate from a survival kit. In it are a few hexamine or fire-lighter blocks, a couple of magic candles, some non-safety matches, and a small flint striker, all padded out with cotton wool. These fire kits can make fire making that much easier in difficult situations, perhaps when you are exhausted and have little tinder to hand.

Remember this

As illustrated in the case study, wet or damp wood can be burned if split open to expose the dry middle. With further axe work, or using a sharp knife, the dry inner wood can be cut out into dry sticks and put on the fire to burn. The outer, damp parts can be placed at the edge of the fire and will dry out as the inner pieces burn. Once your fire is truly alight, place damp wood closer. As it catches, move it in and replace with more wood needing to be dried. The white smoke generated can be a nuisance but will keep away irritating mosquitoes and other flying insects.

Dried animal dung is a common fire-burning material in many parts of the world, particularly where wood is hard to come by. Flattened into discs and then sun-dried, camel, cow and horse dung burns well and has kept desert nomads and others alive and warm for hundreds of years.

Different woods burn differently (oak burns hotter and slower than pine), but in a survival situation, you do not want to waste time and calories seeking out a particular wood, and are usually best off using what is close by. Also, differently shaped fires burn at different rates and can be used for slightly different purposes. For example, a pyramid-shaped fire will burn quicker than a flat fire, which is better suited to balancing pots and for cooking, so a simple pyramid-shaped fire is generally what you want in a survival situation where speed and saving energy are key factors.

Focus points

* Fire has many uses in a survival context, and is not just for cooking.
* Always have plenty of tinder, kindling and larger pieces of wood to hand *before* attempting to light anything.
* Practise lighting a fire with a sparker.
* Practise lighting a fire in the rain, or at least with wet wood in damp conditions.
* Know what makes good tinder, and the methods of igniting it.

Next step

By now you should have understood and acquired the skills needed to find and purify water, and to get a fire going. Now it's time to think about making a shelter. As with all the skills covered in this book, practising this before you are in a survival situation is vital – make sure you do this rather than just learn the theory.

5

Shelter making

In this chapter you will learn:

- ▶ *The benefits of a shelter*
- ▶ *How to build a shelter*
- ▶ *The various factors to consider when building a shelter*
- ▶ *How to choose the best location for your shelter*

Shelters are similar to fires in that they have several uses which may not always appear obvious. For example, a shelter can:

▶ protect from adverse weather: heat, rain/snow or cold

▶ protect from unwanted insects and animals

▶ raise morale

No polar explorer would survive long without being able to retreat into a tent and out of the sub-zero temperatures and heat-draining winds. Desert travellers must also escape extreme conditions; they need to shelter from the blistering sun during the day and the freezing temperatures at night. The protection a shelter offers is not just to make you comfortable, it may be life saving. A shelter may be able to keep you alive and out of harm's way until rescue arrives. It may enable you to conserve calories and/or water until adverse weather retreats and you are able to continue your journey to safety.

All outdoor people ought to know the basics of shelter building. Survival skills are your insurance when things go wrong, and are the skills that keep you alive when disaster strikes.

 Key idea

It is important you understand the benefits of a shelter. You need to build one before you or the situation deteriorates further, and you run out of energy.

In genuine survival situations, shelters should always be constructed with the minimum of effort. Conserve your calories. If food and water are in a limited supply, you do not want to expend so much physical effort building an elaborate shelter, so as to leave yourself exhausted and dehydrated – and perhaps closer to death than you were at the start! Unless food and water are in plentiful supply, always think about energy and water conservation.

Case study

In 1991, 22-year-old trekker James Scott decided to explore the Himalayan foothills. The Himalayas, particularly the section that runs through Nepal, attract thousands of people each year wanting to trek and climb these monumental and magnificent mountains.

As the result of poor weather conditions, Scott lost the trail he was following. A blizzard buried the path completely. Scott turned back, hoping he could retrace his steps, connect up to a small river he had passed, and follow it to a nearby village. Although he found the small river, it led to a steep waterfall, and he could not get to the village.

Scott took shelter from the harsh weather conditions by spending the night under a rocky overhang. Not an ideal camp for the night, but it kept him a little warmer. The next day he tried to push on to the village shown on his map, but he failed to reach it. He was cold and wet, without any water, and his only food was some chocolate. He returned to his shelter.

The shelter protected him from getting any wetter, and enabled him to slowly dry out his clothes. He resorted to sucking snowballs for water and kept reasonably hydrated. Food was a serious problem, but the shelter meant the calories required to stay warm and alive were reduced considerably.

Scott survived for 42 days, and was eventually found by a helicopter and airlifted to safety. Without being able to take shelter Scott would have probably drifted into hypothermia because he was cold, wet and exhausted. He would have died. A shelter, even something primitive and very basic, can make all the difference.

Remember this

Try to utilize natural features as much as possible. Fallen trees, rocky overhangs, caves, vehicles, upturned canoes, etc., should all be used where possible.

It is far more energy efficient to adapt something, than it is to build the whole shelter from scratch. Shelter building often takes hours, and will use up time and calories you may not have too much of. However, a poorly-constructed shelter may quickly fall down in the first wind, or leak cold rain over you. It is a balance. Do not be over ambitious, otherwise your shelter may remain unfinished because of its elaborate design and your lack of materials and energy. All could lower your morale and expose you to the risk of a premature death.

I always carry a waterproof poncho or basha and am able to adapt it to an existing natural feature to create a lean-to, tent or covering of some description. It is very rare that the only shelter possible is to build something requiring all four walls and a roof.

Snow shelters should be trenches or poncho-covered holes, not full-blown igloos. Conserve your energy and do the least amount that you can get away with. There may be nothing to eat for hours or days ahead.

Common shelters

There is no limit to what can be adapted and used as a shelter. Here are some common shelters that have been used many times, and need to be in your 'internal library' to draw upon and customize to your situation.

TRENCHES

In desert and snow conditions, sometimes the only way out of the wind or direct sun is to dig a coffin-like trench and escape the worse of the weather. Cover your trench with whatever you can find: a poncho, a series of sticks or branches, debris, a rucksack (at least over your head), or plastic sheet. Trench digging is only a practical option in snow or desert conditions where you can dig reasonably deep without needing a shovel or something similar – not many hikers and travellers carry a spade! Trying to dig a trench shelter in a forest will be extremely difficult and potentially cost you valuable calories that you may be unable to replace.

SNOW HOLES

If a simple trench is not appropriate for whatever reason, you must still find a means of getting out of the wind and, perhaps, away from life-threatening blizzards. Snow holes have been used frequently by mountaineers and explorers, often when stranded unexpectedly in Arctic-like conditions. Use whatever tools you may have, perhaps an ice axe or ski. Find the lee side of a steep ridge where you are pretty sure the snow is deep. Make sure the entrance is not in direct line with the prevailing wind, otherwise cold wind and snow will blow straight in. Dig a small entrance tunnel for about a metre, then veer off to one side and up. You need to dig out a curve-walled room higher than your entrance, ensuring the roof is also curved. The curved structure is stronger, and also ensures you are not dripped on once the chamber warms up a little. As cold air falls, making the sleeping area slightly higher than your entrance will keep you a little warmer. Block off the entrance with a rucksack or pile of snow. Have regard to ventilation, and don't seal yourself in. Consider poking a small hole through the roof, especially if you cook anything in your shelter.

LEAN-TO

In its simplest form, this might be a series of long sticks propped up against a fallen tree. Cover these poles with dense, leafy branches until the covering is thick enough to prevent or slow down rain coming in. If you have access to thin, bendable sticks, weave them horizontally through the poles first. This will create something stronger and more durable. Hook branches into the panel to make a roof. Block off one end with more sticks and leafy branches. To further improve insulation, and to keep you comfortable, cover the floor with branches or thin sticks. See Figure 5.1 overleaf.

Try it now

Go into a forest and see how many fallen trees you can find that could be adapted to make a simple lean-to. When you are on a hiking trip, get into the habit of spotting potential shelters and practise building them, instead of using your tent.

Figure 5.1 Lean-to shelter using a fallen tree (© Kate Polley)

FRAME LEAN-TO

As an alternative to a lean-to, but using the same basic principles, another easily-made shelter can be built using one upright tree. Dig into the ground a sturdy forked stick about two metres from a tree. Using boot-laces or a branch in the tree, fix a horizontal stick between the two to create a small goal post-like structure. Lay long sticks from the horizontal stick to the ground to make a large wedge-shaped structure. (See Figure 5.2.) As with the simple lean-to, now weave thin sticks into the long sticks to make it more secure. Cover with dense branches to make it waterproof. Block up the sides. In front of the open side, make a fire. Again, to improve comfort and insulation, make a floor of thin sticks, such as birch. In some cases, you may be able to run your horizontal pole between the low branches of two trees, and not have to make an upright. Adapt what you have, and conserve energy.

The shelters described above are simple and practical, and can realistically be made by someone in a true survival situation. Anything more elaborate is probably beyond the means of someone fighting to survive. If you do have a poncho, plastic sheet, etc., then use it as the roof to something, or use a few sticks and turn it into a small tent.

Figure 5.2 Frame lean-to shelter (© Kate Polley)

Location

When you build your shelter, consider all risks, such as what could fall on you (e.g., overhanging branches and rocks). Also, take into account where heavy rain might run – hopefully not straight through your shelter! Shelters built at the bottom of valleys will feel very cold, as cold air descends. Similarly, shelters built on exposed hills may suffer from strong winds and penetrating rain.

Don't rest up too near water as you may be pestered by insects, as well as animals watering. Check the ground and the water's edge for footprints. Shelters built in the snow should have their openings at right-angles to the wind. It is common sense, but in true survival situations thinking straight can be very hard.

In jungles and forests, you really want to get off the ground where at all possible. There are a great many insects, snakes and unwanted animals that might cause you problems, especially at night. In cold conditions, your heat loss will be slowed down if you can reduce direct contact with the ground. However, if you have no option but to lie on the ground, try making a bed of sticks, ferns or leaves. Hard stony ground is made more comfortable if you lie on your front rather than your back. Be wary of lying directly on the sand (either desert or coastal) as heat-seeking insects and scorpions may pay you a visit.

Shelter making is largely down to an individual's imagination and resourcefulness. Around the world, people have established shelters in swamps and marshes by constructing platforms and floating bases; in jungles by using hammocks; in deserts by using tents; in the Arctic using ice-made shelters. Human resourcefulness is without limit.

Fires and shelters boost morale, in addition to any physiological benefit. This psychological effect should not be underestimated.

Remember this

A person survives largely because of the state of their mind, not the state of their body.

Focus points

* Shelters can be vital to survival in adverse weather conditions.
* Conserve your calories and adapt existing natural features before attempting to build anything.
* Have regard to the location before you start making a shelter.
* Shelters, like fires, have an enormous psychological effect, and this alone could keep you alive in a survival situation.

Next step

Now that you have hopefully stabilized your situation and prevented any immediate worsening of your condition, you need to start improving it. Although it is possible to survive without any food for many days, the sooner you start replacing lost calories the better. It is time to rediscover the hunter-gatherer within you.

6

Food

In this chapter you will learn:

▶ *About your calorific and nutritional requirements*

▶ *What the effects of food deprivation are*

▶ *About common sources of the major food groups*

▶ *How to identify common edible plants*

▶ *Hunting techniques*

Key idea

Food is fuel, and although you can go many days on nothing, the need for food must be addressed *before* energy reserves run down and renders you too weak to act constructively. As with most survival skills, a little preparation, practice and clear thinking is all that is required.

Nutritional requirements

An average adult needs around 2,000 calories per day if remaining relatively inactive; approximately 3,500 if active, and probably double this if active in a very cold climate. When you consider that a whole loaf of bread is about 1,800 calories, this can seem a lot to consume in a day. However, you burn around one hundred calories per hour just sitting down.

Ideally you should try to eat a diet with a balance of protein, fats, carbohydrates and the necessary vitamins and minerals. However, in a survival situation which you anticipate lasting no more than a week or two, concentrate on just consuming as many calories as you can. Worry about your long-term health requirements once back home.

Effects of food deprivation

You need food for:

▶ physical energy

▶ mental clarity and drive

▶ the repair of injuries and recovery from illness

▶ warmth: your body temperature will begin to drop if under-nourished and hypothermia could follow

▶ morale: in the right frame of mind you can survive longer and accomplish more

Once existing food reserves have been used up, the effects of food deprivation begin to appear. These include:

- fatigue

- mental indecisiveness and a loss of concentration

- irritability

- depression

- headaches

- continual feeling of cold

- ketosis: this is where body fats start to breakdown due to insufficient carbohydrate intake. This may cause all of the above symptoms including nausea and a difficulty in drinking. It ultimately results in ketone toxicity which can lead to a coma.

Having an insufficient diet can also make you increasingly susceptible to illness as the body's immune system weakens. Although there are stories of people surviving weeks without food, they usually managed to do so by remaining as inactive as possible and hoping they would be found.

Remember this

You should not rely on being rescued and instead take control of the situation by taking positive action before physical weakness and mental instability prevents you from doing so.

Food types and sources

The main types of food you should be concerned with are fats, carbohydrates and protein.

Fats have the highest calorific value but require relatively large amounts of water before they can be digested and absorbed. They provide an excellent source of energy and can be stored to keep you warm, protect body organs and keep the digestive system lubricated. Good examples of foods high in fat are nuts, eggs, fish and animal meat.

Carbohydrates are the most important food type to try and gather. Although they do not contain as many calories as fats, they do not require as much water to be digested and are therefore more easily absorbed into the body. Carbohydrates are a very good source of energy and also help maintain a healthy nervous system. Useful sources that you may encounter if living off the land include fruit, roots, honey and plant tubers.

Protein is responsible for cell growth and repair. As a last resort when nothing else is available, it can be used to generate energy. The complex nature of protein does not, however, make it a particularly efficient source of energy production. Common sources in the wild would be any fish, bird or animal.

Certain plants have some protein content but those that do (e.g. legume seeds, cereals) often require too much preparation to be of much use.

Key idea

The digestion of food requires water. Dehydration will be worsened if you eat without being able to drink. If water is in short supply do not eat unless the food has a high water content, for example a fruit.

Useful preparations

Pack high-calorie foods for the duration of your trip, plus a little extra. Plan your meals in advance and bag up individual portions rather than just bringing a big bag of whatever, believing it to be enough. Bring plenty of tea (avoid coffee because it is a powerful diuretic and therefore unhelpful if suffering from dehydration).

Take into account where you are going to get water and how necessary it will be for your meals. Dehydrated meals are light to pack, but in some circumstances may not be as useful as those that can also be eaten raw or straight out of the can/packet.

Have regard to how you are going to have to cook your food and take the appropriate stoves and pots. I always aim to cook and eat out of a single pot. This means that little of the nutritional value of the food is lost.

Carry a small quantity of curry or chilli powder. If having to eat new foods, you may find them foul-tasting at first. I find sprinkling my worm and slug stew with a little Madras curry powder makes it more edible!

Expand your knowledge and allow your mind and taste buds to accept foreign foods.

Try it now

Supplement your meals on your next hike or camping trip with foods gathered in the wild along the way. Perhaps put some burdock root or dandelion leaves in with the food that you've brought with you. This will lessen the shock and accelerate your ability to adapt should a real survival situation befall you and you have to find every calorie of food yourself.

Plants as a food source

Plants are very easy to gather but the problem is finding them in the first place. You cannot be expected to know the edible plants and methods of preparation for all of the countries that you may find yourself in. The time of year and the geography will also need to be taken into account. Far better to learn a few commonly occurring plants and the edibility test below.

Remember this

As with anything you have to do in a survival situation, always balance energy expenditure against the benefits of your actions. There would be little point in spending a thousand calories retrieving a food source bearing only fifteen calories.

Before you test any plant for edibility, as a rule of thumb, avoid the following:

▶ plants with a milky sap

▶ red or brightly coloured plants

▶ any grasses or plants with tiny barbs on their stems or leaves

▶ any mature or wilting plants

While there will always be exceptions, avoiding the above will generally be safer.

Having taken into account the above, use the test below to check edibility. If you are in a group, make sure only one person tests one plant at a time.

▶ Smell: Crush up a small portion of the plant and smell it. Discard it if it smells of either bitter almonds or peaches.

▶ Look: Avoid old or slimy plants as they may have become toxic or of depleted nutritional value. Generally speaking, the newer parts of the plant are better and safer.

▶ Irritability: Squeeze some of the plant's juices on to your lower forearm or inside your elbow joint. Discard if any rash or irritability occurs.

▶ Mouth test: Put a small portion on the inside of your bottom lip, chew a little but do not swallow. Put under your tongue for a few minutes. Discard if you feel any burning or stinging.

▶ Eat some: Eat a small amount if all the above steps have proved okay. Ideally, wait around eight hours to see if there are any adverse reactions, sickness or diarrhoea, etc.

If your plant (it does not apply to fungi) passes the test, you can add it to your food stock. Remember, you are after plants that produce a high quantity of energy. The best parts of plant to gather are the roots, the seeds and the fruit. The leaves may have medicinal value and a nice flavour, but our priority here is calories.

EXAMPLES OF EDIBLE PLANTS
In the tropics you have the widest choice. Palms, bamboos, nuts, sugarcanes and fruits such as mangoes, persimmons and apples are relatively common.

In desert regions of the world you will be reliant on plants like baobabs, prickly pears, wild gourds and acacias.

In the Arctic you'll have to rely on lichens, spruces and willows, although in the summer months many temperate region plants are also available.

The temperate zone offers us an abundance of edible plants, including dandelions (leaves and roots), young bracken fronds, red or white clover leaves, watercress (leaves and stems), sorrel (leaves and shoots) and hawthorn (young shoots and fruit). The leaves of nettles are high in iron, and make a good tea too. Boil briefly to remove the sting. Two especially useful plants quite well loaded with carbohydrates are:

Cat-tail: can be found beside many slow-moving freshwater rivers or lakes and is easily identified as the tall reed (up to five metres) with a brown sausage-shaped flower head. It is the rope-like rhizome roots under the water and at the end of the plant that you need. Break them into 30-centimetre lengths and scrape them clean. You can either eat them raw or char them on a fire first. Tear apart and suck out the carbohydrate-rich pulp.

Burdock: occurs in most woodlands and can be recognized by the large green heart-shaped leaves. Dig up the fat roots and clean up before eating raw. These roots have a high carbohydrate content. See Figure 6.1.

Figure 6.1 Burdock leaf (© Helen Polley)

Animals as a food source

Key idea

With energy, anything is possible. Your survival invariably depends on whether you have sufficient mental and physical energy to either endure hardship, or reach safety. Energy means food. Food is fuel and it will keep you warm and keep you going. Although plants are easy to collect, they can be difficult to identify, make edible, and to find at certain times of the year. Birds, fish and animals are with us all year round and are easy to identify and prepare. The problem is, they don't like being caught.

FISH

Fish are an excellent source of calories and full of protein and fats as well as useful vitamins and minerals. There are two main ways of catching them: trapping and angling.

Trapping – if the water runs shallow and you can see the fish, this method can work well. Dam up the river with rocks or logs and channel the water through a route narrow enough to net, spear or even scoop the fish out.

Angling – if you have some line (e.g. a length of paracord), tie on a hook (or safety pin, thorn, piece of wire) and bait with whatever you can find. The following tips might help:

▶ Avoid casting a shadow over the water and instead sit or lie down. Fish are wary of movement on the bank and can see you more easily than you can see them.

▶ Fishing at night (perhaps attracting fish with a torch) or early mornings are often the best times.

▶ In hotter weather, fish often seek shade under overhanging trees or by the shadowed parts of the riverbank. Deeper, calmer waters are often preferred.

▶ In cooler weather, fish may frequent shallower parts of the river, perhaps near the river's edge or the surface.

▶ Look for fish breaking the water's surface trying to catch insects.

- Berries, insects, snails, crabs, worms and frogs all make excellent bait. Dig around the bank. Moving, live bait is normally preferred but don't rule out the use of shiny lures.

- Pre-baiting the area by tossing in surplus bait may make the fish less cautious of your baited hook.

- Your hooked fish is likely to struggle most as it leaves the water, so be ready to help it out by lifting it in a net or container.

- Fish can also be caught by suspending baited lines tied onto a branch or cord at varying lengths, spanning the river. However, this method only really works if you are using proper fishing hooks and strong line that the fish cannot free themselves from with a struggle.

▶ Preparation

First, kill the fish with a sharp blow to the head. If it is a very scaly fish, de-scale it as best you can by scraping your knife in a tail–to-head direction. Fish putrefy fairly quickly, so prepare it and eat it as soon as you can.

Wash the fish as best you can and carefully slit it open along the underside by cutting from the anus to just behind the gills. Don't cut too deeply or you will damage the internal organs and everything will get very messy. Remove all the organs and wash it as best as you can. Remove the head and tail. If is a large fish, try removing the spine and ribs although this is normally easier once the fish is cooked. Remove the outer skin on larger fish if you can.

Fish can be cooked easily and quickly. Fish stew is my preference as it ensures nothing of nutritional value is lost and anything else caught or collected can be added to the pot. A pinch of curry powder can mask any nasty tastes if necessary. If you don't have a pot, try cooking it over an open fire, perhaps skewered on a green stick.

BIRDS

Birds are another good source of food and can be caught by combining fishing techniques with animal snares and traps. Common methods of catching birds are:

- **Spearing and catapulting:** Sharpen a long straight stick and try spearing larger, slower-moving birds such as gulls and pigeons. Consider making a sling-shot or catapult to fire stones at birds, in order to stun them.

- **Deadfall trap:** Use a stick to prop up one side of a heavy weight. Tie a length of string to the stick and then put bait under the weight. Hide out of sight and use the string to pull the stick away once your prey is positioned sufficiently under the weight to become trapped or killed by it. If you had a box, you could use this instead of a heavy weight. See Figure 6.2.

- **Snares set up on branches:** Where possible, secure small snares along larger branches, baited with whatever food scraps you have. Larger birds may get their feet caught in a looped snare, and the harder they pull away, the tighter the snare becomes.

- **Baited hooks:** Attach a thin line to a hook and bury this into a piece of bait. Toss the bait at the bird. When the bird swallows the bait the hook should snag enabling you to pull the bird in. This method works best with water birds such as gulls and ducks.

▶ Preparation

Break the bird's neck. The sooner you start plucking the easier it is. Pouring hot water over the area being plucked will loosen the feathers a little – unless it's a water bird in which case the

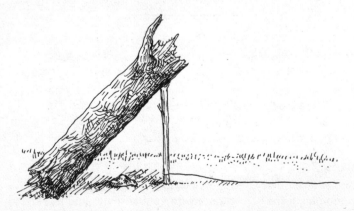

Figure 6.2 A deadfall trap (© Kate Polley)

feathers will tighten. Remove the head and hang the body up by its feet. Carefully slit open and remove the internal organs. Cut the flesh into smaller pieces, which can be cooked in a stew. Save any waste for bait. Avoid eating birds raw or consuming their blood as parasitic infections are common.

MAMMALS

In my experience, elaborate traps requiring numerous bits of wood and metres of paracord are not always appropriate for the starved survivor to construct, particularly if they have limited tools and energy.

Larger game (e.g. deer) can be very difficult to catch. Try hiding in places frequented by the animals, such as watering holes and well-worn animal trails. Kill using an improvised spear or bow and arrow, made from whatever materials you can find. You will need several arrows/spears to bring down a large animal. Follow tracks and try to remain camouflaged. Keep upwind, out of sight and quiet. First and last light are usually the best times to hunt, as this is when a great many animals are most active and leave their burrows and hides.

Snares are normally more appropriate for smaller animals and are simple, easy to set, and offer a reasonable rate of success. They are small wire loops that will tighten around the prey's neck and will not loosen in a struggle. The free end must be very securely tied to a heavy stick or pegged into the ground, otherwise the animals will run off with the snare. See Figure 6.3.

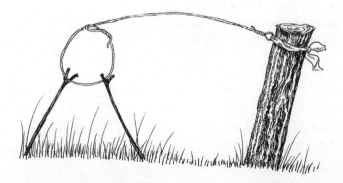

Figure 6.3 A basic snare (© Kate Polley)

To enhance your success:

▶ Always make a note of where you have set the snare.

▶ The snare should be three to four fingers height off the ground and about a fist width wide.

▶ Secure the snare well as the captured animal will try its hardest to escape.

▶ Do not walk on the animal paths – your scent will scare the animals away.

▶ Try to wear gloves and minimize your contact with the actual snare; again your scent will alert your prey to your presence.

▶ Try to direct your prey towards your snare, perhaps by repositioning heavy rocks or logs.

▶ Check snares regularly as caught animals may be eaten by other animals or may even manage to free themselves given enough time.

▶ Always be conscious of your scent and reduce any disturbances to the surrounding area.

▶ Site the snare along animal trails or near dens but don't set them too close to the burrow or den as animals are most alert as they approach or leave their home.

▶ Preparation

Approaching a caught or cornered animal can be very dangerous so exercise caution. Slit the animal's throat to make sure that it is dead. Remove the skin as best you can by carefully cutting and pulling away from the muscle. Gut the animal by cutting from the anus up to the chin. Don't cut too deep or you will slice the stomach and internal organs and there will be an awful mess. Remove all of the internal organs and retain as bait for your next fishing or hunting attempt.

Cut the meat into smaller pieces for your stew, or barbecue over a fire if you do not have a pot.

Note that as rabbit meat lacks certain vitamins and minerals, when eaten by humans, the body has to use its own stored nutrients to digest it. If you continue to eat rabbit alone over a long period, you risk illness and even death.

OTHER ANIMALS TO CONSIDER

Grasshoppers: remove the soft bits from the hard shell and eat raw.

Caterpillars and larvae: skewer and cook like a kebab. Avoid hairy or brightly coloured varieties.

Worms: starve for 24 hours to purge them of anything unpleasant. Then cut them up into small pieces to put in a stew. Alternatively dry them out in an empty pot over a fire, then grind them into a powder to thicken a stew.

Slugs: cook on a skewer like caterpillars.

Snails: lay them on hot embers, shell opening uppermost for about five to ten minutes. You can also starve them for a few days then eat them after boiling for about 20 minutes. Avoid brightly coloured varieties.

Avoid grubs found on the underside of leaves or anything that feeds on dung.

Case study

The survival of Ricky Megee is incredible. In January 2006 Ricky gave three men a lift while travelling through a remote part of the Australian Outback. The landscape was featureless and desolate. Ricky was passing through during the summer time and it was hot and dry; temperatures commonly rose to the forties.

The three men were not what they seemed. They offered Ricky a drink, which turned out to be drugged. Once he was unconscious, they stripped him of his footwear, stole his car and everything he had. They left him for dead in a ditch, under a sheet of plastic weighed down with rocks.

Feeling confused and groggy, Ricky eventually came round. From a small hill, he could see that the road stretched as far as the horizon in both directions, and that there were no buildings anywhere to be seen. He had no water or food, and it was very hot. For several days he survived on nothing but sips of his own urine, and slurps from a puddle left after a storm. After walking for miles with torn feet in the blistering heat, Ricky came upon a stream. He drank and rested. It was now six days since he had been drugged and mugged.

Ricky realized he needed food to last much longer. He caught a lizard, stuck it on a stick, and let the hot sun dry it out. He ate it, and soon took to insects, leeches, and frogs too. He undertook a simplified version of the plant edibility test, and ate some plant material where he could. Combined, these few calories kept him alive. His body weight was, however, dropping rapidly.

Lack of food and the unlikelihood of a passing car, forced him to move on. He walked more than another 50 miles to a water hole, occasionally collapsing on the way. Although he passed no people, he came across an abandoned cattle station, and made himself a shelter from the life-sapping heat. He stayed there for another seven weeks.

He survived on sun-dried lizards and frogs, and water from the water hole he had found. He had to contend with a poisonous spider bite, ever-circling dingoes looking for an easy meal, and a potentially life-threatening tooth abscess. He survived the spider bite, scared off the dingoes, and pulled out the infected tooth with a piece of wire and a key. Desperate as his situation was, Ricky would not lie down and die.

In April, two ranchers passing by found him by chance. His condition shocked them; he looked like a skeleton, but was unbelievably still alive. He had dropped from 105 kilos to 48 kilos, losing around half his body weight during the ordeal. He had survived 71 days on his own, living off the land and eating whatever he could catch. He was taken to hospital, and slowly nursed back to health.

A full account of the story can be read in *Left for Dead in the Outback* by Ricky Megee.

To reduce the shock of killing and gutting something for the first time, try doing so before you need to. You can't allow squeamishness to compromise your chances of survival. Although your survival is often hinged upon good preparations and physical strength, it often relies on a state of mind too. A 'who dares wins' attitude in which outrageous acts and doing the unexpected, may be just as vital. Many survivors have survived by eating animals they would have previously found repellent (see the case study above).

Remember this

Catching live food is never as easy as it sounds. To maximize your chances, you must simultaneously put into place as many techniques as possible. Set animal snares and fishing lines as well as bird snares and fish traps. Then start gathering your edible plants, slugs, snails, etc. You should not rely on one method alone.

Take calorie conservation seriously. Don't expend more calories catching your prey than you will ultimately gain from it.

As with most survival skills, you are well advised to practise fishing, hunting and trapping skills well before you need to rely on them. Read Chapter 12 on tracking and one or more of the guides on wild foods and plant identification referred to in Appendix 4 (Taking things further).

Focus points

* Address the need for food before you are too weak to do anything about it.
* Digestion requires water, so do not eat dry food without having water available.
* Learn the plant edibility test, as well as a few commonly found edible plants in the area you are visiting.
* Use as many techniques for catching live food as possible – don't rely on just one method.
* Learn how to prepare fish, birds and animals for eating.

Next step

Although you should now know how to stay alive and prevent any further deterioration of your condition, you need to get back to safety. For a variety of reasons, staying put often offers you a greater chance of survival than moving on. You therefore need to be able to signal to rescuers and others, and attract attention.

7

Signalling

In this chapter you will learn:

▶ *How being able to signal can save your life*
▶ *Methods of visual signalling*
▶ *Methods of signalling using sound*
▶ *About the need to plan ahead*

Being able to signal for help can be essential to your survival in many cases. There may be situations where you can't always walk to safety – injury, insufficient provisions, too great a distance, etc. If stranded with a vehicle (car, aircraft, etc.) the general advice is to stay with the vehicle. In these circumstances, you need to be able to signal to any rescuers or people who may be in the area.

To greatly increase your chances of being found, it would help enormously if someone knew you were lost in the first place. Before you leave your home, Youth Hostel, hotel, etc., let someone know your destination, intended route and estimated timescale. Ask them to raise the alarm if they do not hear from you by a certain time. This way at least a search and rescue operation can be mounted, rather than heading off to the forests or mountains without anyone knowing where you are going. If you are lying injured, it will help if someone knows you are missing, and roughly where to look.

When heading off into the wilderness, be it a desert, a jungle, or a mountain range, always take a means of signalling for help to guide rescuers to you. In some situations, your life expectancy may be measured in days or hours, and time may be crucial: help them to help you.

 Key idea

Plan ahead, anticipate the unexpected, and take a means of calling or signalling for help if an accident befalls you or your group. Not everything goes to plan.

Signalling is essentially based on two methods: sight and sound – get yourself seen or get yourself heard.

Sound

Trying to signal using sound is probably the method that first comes to mind for most people: we simply shout 'help!' Using some form of loud noise as a means of getting noticed is appropriate at night or when visibility is poor and the distance from a potential rescuer is not too far. You should consider using the following as methods of attracting attention:

Emergency transmitter beacons: These are now readily available from many outdoor shops, and are strongly recommended to those climbing or skiing in areas where avalanches are a risk. As long as you have someone monitoring you back home, you should also consider taking one on any trip to a remote area. The moment you signal for help, a swift rescue operation can be put into action.

The watchmakers, Breitling, make a watch called the Professional Emergency with a built-in emergency transmitter. Using a tiny 121.5 MHz transmitter it sends a distress signal to the search and rescue services and guides them to the location of the watch. The crew of the Mata Rangi raft expedition used such a watch when in trouble at sea, and were all rescued. It has also been successfully used by several other stranded adventurers. Remember, however, that all emergency beacons will have a finite battery life and range. Check that both suit your trip before taking one.

Whistle: Six blasts means help, repeat every minute. An emergency rescue whistle should always be carried by those in mountain and jungle conditions, as visibility is often very limited in these places, and any rescue signal usually has to involve sound rather than sight.

Try it now

Buy a whistle; they are cheap and easy to carry, and should form part of your standard outdoor kit wherever you go. Many outdoor shops and suppliers sell rescue whistles which are designed to be especially loud and can emit a sound in excess of 120 decibels. See the case study below.

Mobile telephone: Often very convenient and frequently carried – but they have limitations. In many areas there will simply be no signal, and the duration of your trip (or incident) may exceed the battery life of your phone. Mobile phones are not that robust or waterproof, and may be damaged and put out of operation quite easily. It may still be difficult for rescuers to find you unless you know exactly where you are, and can guide them to you. Still worth carrying, but have regard to its limitations, and take a spare battery or emergency charger.

Any repeated sound pattern will probably draw attention. You need not worry about tapping out a message in Morse Code. Making a loud noise, over and over, should attract attention. Like whistle blasts, bursts of six anything will help.

Energy, whether yours or a battery, will be expended trying to signal for help using sound. You will have to decide whether that energy is being used wisely, or should be held back for a better use, or at a better time. Pause for thought before you run out of energy.

Case study

Colorado has long been a favourite destination of skiers. It is a vast area, offering opportunities to get away from it all, and enjoy peace and solitude. Charles Horton was 55, and had been doing some cross-country skiing in the Steamboat Springs area. After a couple of miles and a light lunch, he was ready to head back to his car and off home. However, he slipped awkwardly, and sustained a serious injury to his leg. His knee was shattered and he could barely move.

Horton was at about 9,000 feet above sea level, and nobody would be looking for him for quite a while. Friends who knew where he was, had gone away for a few days. He was more or less immobile, exposed to sub-zero temperatures, and death was surely close by. He crawled to the shelter of some nearby pines and managed to make a fire with some matches he had in a jacket pocket. Horton tried to sleep but it was difficult as the temperature dropped.

Horton had nothing to eat and only snow to quench his thirst. Painful hours became exhausting and unbearable days. He had no means of moving and no food. After a week clinging to life, a blizzard blew in and covered him with more than six inches of snow; it made him virtually invisible to any overheard search teams. It seemed all was lost. However, on the eighth day Horton heard the blasts of a whistle – he immediately responded by blowing his own emergency whistle that he carried with him. He was found.

Had Charles Horton not been able to attract the attention of the searchers, he would surely have died. Carrying something as small as a whistle saved his life.

Sight

Using something visual is appropriate where rescuers/locals are not necessarily close by, and where visibility is at least reasonable. In some cases, such as the desert, you will have no choice but to use a visual aid to attract attention. Consider one or more of the following to get yourself noticed.

Strobe beacons: These are very bright flashing lights that will last hours, if not days, and are often waterproof. Many life-jackets have them built-in and they automatically switch on in water. They make useful rescue aids if among mountain areas, but not always in jungles where the dense vegetation hides most things at ground level.

Fire: Probably one of the most common methods of signalling. Smoke and fire can be seen from a great distance, but virtually anything can be burned to produce a life-saving signal. To emphasize that your fire is in fact a call for help, build three fires in a triangle. This is an internationally recognized distress sign, and should alert any aircraft flying overhead.

Remember this

If you have a choice, build a fire that will produce smoke to contrast your background. Wet wood produces white smoke, and is therefore useful against dark backgrounds like dense forest. Burning something oil based such as rubber or plastic produces black smoke, and works well against light backgrounds such as snow.

Electric torches: Conserve your battery power where you can, but if you believe someone may be able to see you, flash them repeatedly. As with sound, six flashes with a break, repeated over and over, should alert people to the need to at least investigate the source.

Using a camera flash: You could also use a vehicle's lights. Again have regard to battery life, but can be used to attract attention if you have nothing else. Repeated flashes should arouse curiosity, and hopefully draw attention.

Flares: There are many types, both hand-held types and rocket types that shoot off high into the air. Some are very bright and burn magnesium, others produce coloured smoke. Ideal in many cases, as long as someone is close enough to see it, and curious enough to come closer. If you can, carry several, but you are unlikely to get them onto an aircraft so will have to obtain them in the country you are travelling in.

Mirrors: Purpose-made heliographs can be cheaply bought nowadays from most outdoor shops. They are simply mirrors, often with a small hole in the middle. The idea is that you reflect the sun onto a passing aircraft, or someone far off in the distance. In practice, you need to be able to see a potential rescuer, and accurately aim the mirror at them so they get flashed, and then hope they understand it as a rescue signal. Try using anything shiny, but understand the limits of this method.

Large signs: If you believe aircraft will be flying over, perhaps part of a search, you can help them find you by creating a large X or SOS out of stones, or whatever you have to hand.

Remember this

To maximize your chances of being seen, employ several of the above methods simultaneously. Never rely on one method alone. For example, have a bright smoky fire burning or ready to ignite, but also have a gigantic X made out of rocks or debris around you.

Remember this

Always stay with your downed aircraft, broken-down vehicle, etc. You will be easier to find than if you were a lone person wandering in a giant wilderness. From the air you will be invisible, but a car or crashed aircraft will be seen from thousands of metres. In a great many situations, staying with the broken-down/crashed vehicle offers a better chance of survival, for many reasons, than walking off in the hope of reaching safety.

In snowy conditions you could try digging a large X-shaped trench, or SOS. Staining the snow (e.g. with potassium permanganate) or setting light to something that produces dark smoke are also options. Ideally you should prepare for disaster and carry a proper rescue beacon like many skiers do. Even a small emergency-only mobile phone could save your life. Plan ahead.

Smoke in jungle or forest conditions easily becomes dispersed and will not help attract a rescuer. Instead, go to a clearing and allow the smoke out of the forest canopy. Alternatively, make a small raft and build a smoky fire on it, then push it out into a body of water or a river, retaining its position with a length of rope. The smoke should be able to escape the forest and be seen for miles around.

Remember this

You can't predict the future, but you can prepare for it.

Focus points

* Always plan for an accident or break-down, and pack a means of signalling for help.
* Carry a rescue whistle with you at all times.
* Think of ways of attracting attention using sound *and* something visual.
* Use more than one method of signalling simultaneously.
* If stranded in a vehicle, stay with it – a vehicle/aircraft is far easier to see from the air.

Next step

One of the most common reasons for death or disaster is getting lost. You end up somewhere hostile, run out of water, food or fuel, and cannot get back to safety fast enough. Minor injuries suddenly become serious and perhaps life threatening. Good navigation skills are essential to anyone venturing outdoors, and yours should be continually sharpened.

8

Navigation

In this chapter you will learn:

- ▶ *Basic navigation using a map and compass*
- ▶ *How to make an improvised compass*
- ▶ *How to use the sun to find north*
- ▶ *How to use the stars and moon to find north*
- ▶ *The essence of 'natural navigation'*
- ▶ *Methods of measuring distance*

Poor navigation is all too often the reason for avoidable difficulties, and even death. Footpaths seem very clear at the beginning of a trail, then slowly fade to nothing, or bad weather obscures them. The hiker takes the wrong direction, and soon becomes lost. Once lost, more time than planned for is needed to get back to safety. Provisions start to run low, hypothermia or an injury suddenly become very serious concerns. People die every year in Britain alone because poor navigation leads them into situations that they cannot get out of safely. Do not underestimate the need to be a good navigator; it can get you out of trouble quickly and safely. Death and injury are nature's way of dealing with the foolish and ill-prepared.

Basic map and compass work

In Britain, Ordnance Survey (OS) produce extremely accurate maps of every inch of the country. Each map carries a definition of the symbols used and the scale. Learn the common symbols, especially the gradients so you know the steepness of the land. Also note the symbols used for swamps, rivers and features that could prove a danger, such as quicksand and disused mines. Note the age of the map. Plan your route ahead, note the features you should be encountering, and estimate the distance you are likely to cover each day. Before you set off, study your map and find suitable campsites, water refilling points, and the nearest places rescue or help might be sought if an accident occurs.

All OS maps are drawn with north at the top, with trees being shown growing upwards to north. South will therefore be downwards, with east to the right and west to the left. Non-OS maps will have the north point shown, often with north at the top of the map like British OS maps, but not always – make sure you check this.

Remember this

Memorize your route as best you can, and know the general direction in which you are going. This information may be vital if your map and compass become lost or damaged and you have to improvise and go to 'Plan B'. This is especially important if you are on a ship or aircraft, and a serious accident occurs forcing you to fend for yourself.

Maps should not be treated as ever wholly accurate. They are snapshots of how things were when the cartographers drew up the maps, probably years ago. Maps are a guide, and may differ from what is actually on the ground when you are there. There may well be clear footpath tracks shown on the map, but the map may be old and the footpath overgrown through lack of use when you arrive to start a hiking trip. Snow or fog may hide the path completely. You may mistakenly follow an animal trail rather than a footpath because the animal trail is coincidentally near the desired footpath shown on the map. You may not realize this error until hours and miles of hiking in the wrong direction.

Compass navigation is a skill that you should learn to trust, and maps are something you should learn to question. Find where you are on the map, find your destination, and follow the method below to ensure you allow the compass to guide you.

Try it now

Assuming you have a compass with a small rectangular base-plate (see Figure 8.1), lay your compass on the map with the edge of the compass base-plate along the first section of your intended route. Ensure the 'Direction of Travel' arrow (often marked at one end of the base-plate) points along your route towards the destination.

Now rotate the compass housing, or wheel, until the N on the dial points to north on the map (north being at the top of the map). Check that the red/black (north–south) lines in the round part of the compass housing are parallel with the map's lines that run from top to bottom.

Finally, pick up the compass from the map, hold it level in your hand and turn yourself around until the red end of the compass needle (which always points north) coincides with the N on the dial and the large red arrow in the bottom of the round compass housing. The front of the compass base-plate, with the 'Direction of Travel' arrow, is now pointing towards your destination. Keep the needle and dial N aligned, and walk in the direction of the base-plate arrow.

As your route twists and turns you will need to recheck your direction of travel. Simply repeat the steps above, and reset the compass slightly each time. In some cases, a prominent landmark – e.g. a mountain or feature that will be unchanged if the map is old (bridges and forests come and go) – may be able to guide you in the right direction, but check your compass heading frequently in case you have to detour around a marsh or other obstacle.

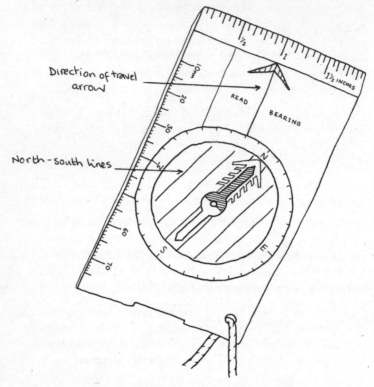

Figure 8.1 Compass with a rectangular base-plate (© Kate Polley)

Carry maps in waterproof map cases, and wear your compass around your neck. Check them frequently, and do not just plod on regardless because it is too much of a hassle to verify your position and heading.

When things go wrong

Navigation equipment – maps, compasses, GPS – get damaged, get lost or simply are not to hand at times. It happens, that's life. Know the route, know how to find north if all your compasses are lost or damaged. However, to minimize your risk, carry spares. If you are on the kind of trip where maps and compasses are going to be crucial, carry spares of everything. Take duplicate maps, and a couple of compasses.

Remember this

The more you can carry in your head, the less you have to carry in your pack.

Always aim to remove risk by planning ahead. Always know the general direction in which you are heading and the approximate distance to a safe place – which may or may not be your destination. If you have no idea in what direction you were travelling, or where the nearest town is, when disaster strikes your situation will be made all the more difficult. Being able to determine north will be of no value to you unless you know in what direction you will find safety. Ignorance kills.

Try it now

Put small back-up compasses into the pockets of your outdoor clothing, perhaps your commonly worn jacket. Only use them if your main compass is not available.

Casio, Suunto, Tissot and Timex all produce wristwatches with built-in compasses. Wear one. Buy a combined compass and thermometer zip pull, and clip it onto your jacket. Many mobile phones have compasses as a downloadable app. By always having a back-up you will hopefully reduce the need to employ the navigation methods below and stay accurately on course. Prevention is better than cure.

If you know what direction to head in but do not have a compass, you should consider either making an improvised compass, or using one of the many natural signs and features to point you in the right direction.

Case study

The story of how the explorer Ernest Shackleton escaped from Antarctica is an example of how superb navigation skills can save lives.

The Imperial Trans-Antarctic Expedition was led by Shackleton in 1914, and involved a team of 27 travelling on board the *Endurance*, intending to walk to the South Pole and to cross Antarctica on foot. Things did not go to plan, and their progress was halted by frozen seas before they reached their jumping off point. They became trapped and could not turn back and get out. Eventually the ice moved in around them and began slowly crushing the ship. Shackleton quickly salvaged a few lifeboats, as much food and provisions as possible, and abandoned the damaged ship. The ice was relentless and finally exerted enough pressure on the ship to break it up; water rushed in and pulled it under the semi-frozen sea.

Shackleton and his team made it to the temporary safety of the pack ice, but clearly could not remain there forever. Between November 1915 and April 1916, the team clung to life and slowly moved north. They hiked at times, but also rowed, drifted and sailed their lifeboats through icy seas and semi-solid ice floes to Elephant Island. At least now they were on solid ground rather than ice that could crack or melt beneath them. However, the island was uninhabited, away from any shipping routes, and it would be a matter of time before provisions ran out and they all died. They had already eaten their dogs.

There was a whaling station about 920 miles away at Stromness on the island of South Georgia. Shackleton decided to leave most of the men on Elephant Island with the bulk of the food and provisions, and take a few men with him to try and get help. If their energy and navigation were good enough, and the sea, storms and starvation bearable, it could be done. The alternative was a slow death on Elephant Island.

The life raft was not made for such a journey, but their navigation was second to none, and Shackleton steered them through 920 miles of ferocious weather and savage seas to South Georgia. It took them more than two weeks; it was an unbelievable feat. Unfortunately, they landed on the other side of the island from where the inhabitants were based, so they had to walk all the way across, more than 30 miles, to Stromness and the whaling station. From here, Shackleton organized a rescue ship and went back for his team still stranded on Elephant Island. Everyone was rescued.

If their navigation had been out, even by a degree or two, Shackleton and his team would have missed South Georgia, and been lost in a desolate sea. All would have perished. Although excellent navigation skills were just one of the attributes that kept Shackleton and his team alive when things went wrong, 27 men owed their lives to the good use of a compass on this occasion.

IMPROVISED COMPASSES

By magnetizing a pin, needle, nail, razor blade, etc. you can make an improvised compass. Dismantle a radio's loudspeaker and remove the magnet. Stroke your needle in one direction only with the same part of the magnet. If stroking towards the point, the point should indicate north when floated on a piece of paper/leaf in a puddle, or bowl of salt-free water. You will need to top up the magnetism regularly. Not always practical, but store it as a possible solution if the problem arises.

You can achieve the same results by stroking a needle or pin with a piece of silk too. The charge will be weak, and need regular topping up, but it can work as a short-term compass.

If you have a battery (at least two volts) and some electric wire, you can polarize a pin, needle or nail electrically. The wire should be insulated. If it is not insulated, you can still use it but wrap the pin/needle in a thin strip of paper to prevent contact. Form a coil with the wire, and then touch its ends to the battery's terminals. Repeatedly insert one end of the pin/needle in and out of the wire coil. The needle will become an electromagnet, and when floated on a small piece of paper or wood in water, it will align itself with a north–south line.

Remember this

All magnetic compasses, especially improvised ones, will be influenced by metal, mobile phones, and magnets around them. Stand well clear of any such materials when using your compass.

SOLAR NAVIGATION

The sun can assist you in direction-finding by two main means:

Shadow tip method: push a stick into the ground and with a stone mark the tip of where the shadow falls. This first stone will

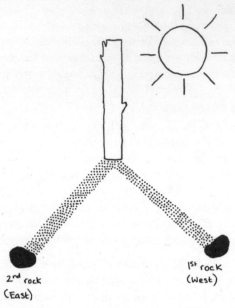

2nd rock (East)

1st rock (West)

Figure 8.2 Direction-finding using the shadow tip method (© Jennifer Polley)

ultimately mark the west point. Wait about 20 minutes and mark the shadow tip again with another stone. This second stone will mark the east point. By knowing the east and west points, you can now mark north and south accordingly. See Figure 8.2.

Wristwatch method: set your watch to local time if you have not done so already. Point the hour hand at the sun. To aid accuracy, hold a small stick beside your watch and let it cast a shadow along the hour hand. At exactly the halfway point between the 12 and the hour hand, draw an imaginary line. North will be the end furthest from the sun. To check yourself, face what you think is north, and the sun (before midday) should be on your right, and on your left after midday. See Figure 8.3.

In the southern hemisphere, point the 12 at the sun instead. Divide the gap between the hour hand and the 12, and north will be at the end *nearest* the sun.

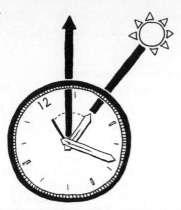

Figure 8.3 Finding north using the wristwatch method (© Kate Polley)

Try it now

Practise using these two solar navigation techniques now. They are very useful and easy to use once you've got the hang of them. Don't worry if you've got a digital watch, just draw a watch face on a piece of paper showing the correct time. Check against a compass to see if you have correctly identified north

LUNAR NAVIGATION

If the night is clear enough to see the moon, it can be used in two ways to help identify north:

1 Draw an imaginary line connecting the tips of the crescent of a moon. Follow this line down to the horizon. The point at which your line touches the horizon will indicate south if you are in the northern hemisphere and north if you are in the southern hemisphere.

2 The second method relies on your knowing the local time and either a full moon or the first quarter moon being visible. The method acknowledges the movement of the moon as it crosses the night sky and works as follows:

▷ At 6 pm: If the first quarter is visible, you will be in the south; if a full moon is visible, you will be in the east.

▷ At 9 pm: If the first quarter is visible, you will be in the southwest; if a full moon is visible, you will be in the southeast.

▷ At midnight: If the first quarter is visible, you will be in the west; if a full moon is visible, you will be in the south.

▷ At 3 am: If the first quarter is visible, you will be in the southwest; if a full moon is visible, you will be in the southeast.

▷ At 6 am: If the first quarter is visible, you will be in the west; if a full moon is visible, you will be in the south.

Generally speaking, you ought not to travel through potential hazardous and unknown country at night, particularly if it is mountainous. The risk of injury is simply too great. Better to locate north, and then mark the ground with sticks or stones, so that in the morning you know which direction to head in.

ASTRAL NAVIGATION

The stars have long been a guide for travellers, and are as reliable today as they always were. In the northern hemisphere, north can be found by locating Polaris, the Pole Star. This is easily found by identifying the Plough (also known as the Big Dipper), which looks like a pan with a long handle. See Figure 8.4 – the two right-hand stars point towards Polaris, which is the main star in the constellation Ursa Minor.

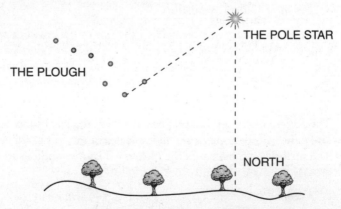

Figure 8.4 The Plough (Big Dipper) and the Pole Star (© Kate Polley)

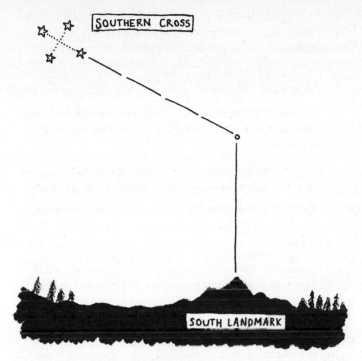

Figure 8.5 The Southern Cross (© Kate Polley)

In the southern hemisphere you need to identify the five-starred Southern Cross. Follow the longer line of stars down by about 4–5 lengths towards the ground. From this point in the sky, drop down to earth: this is south (see Figure 8.5.)

Apart from the Pole Star, stars move and their movement can also assist you in direction finding. For example, pick a star and gauge its travel by lining it up with a fixed marker, like the tip of a fence post. Watch as the star moves.

If your star:

▶ keeps to the right, you are roughly facing south

▶ keeps to the left, you are roughly facing north

▶ rises, you are facing east

▶ descends, you are facing west

As mentioned under lunar navigation, night travel is not usually recommended. Once you have identified north, and therefore the direction you need to travel in, make an arrow out of stones or sticks on the ground and set off in this direction at first light. Pick out something ahead of you that is in line with your direction of travel, and aim for it.

NATURAL NAVIGATION

Natural navigation is the term given to finding your direction based upon observations of the night sky, the position of the sun, the movements of animals and birds, the shape of the landscape, the way plants and flowers grow and move, and wind direction.

Wind: By knowing the direction of the prevailing wind you can get a rough idea of where the compass points are. Note the effects of wind on grasses, isolated trees, sand dunes etc. and use this to estimate the direction.

Vegetation: Most northern hemisphere plants turn to face the sun and by midday many are facing south. Again, check them against your compass on your next trip, and before an accident occurs. Build up a good knowledge of how the plants are orientated in the area you are exploring. Some mosses prefer the damp and grow more prolifically on the northern side of rocks and plants. This is a rough guide, but it may help. If you come across cut down trees, note the lines on the exposed stump. The more spaced-out lines indicate greater growth than the closely-packed lines. The south-facing side usually grows more than the sheltered northern side. A tree or bush will have more branches and be slightly heavier on one side, the south facing side.

Birds: If you are near the coast, the flight patterns of sea birds can help. They generally fly out to sea in the mornings, find some fish to eat, etc., and then return to land in the late afternoon. If you are heading for the coast because you know help to be there, these movements can be helpful. During migration periods, you may be able to see great flocks of birds heading south to warmer climes.

Key idea

Natural navigation is about observation, and using several observations to form an opinion as to the direction. It would be unsafe to use one observation alone to make an important decision.

DISTANCE MEASURING

Knowing how far you have travelled from a known point will help in estimating your position. In the absence of landmarks to pinpoint yourself by, you have to consider other methods. The most common of these are:

Pace counting: By knowing how many strides it takes you to walk a mile, or kilometre, count them off as you walk and clock up the number of miles/kilometres by using knotted string, or moving pebbles from one pocket to another, etc. Alternatively, use an electronic or mechanical pedometer instead; this is an accurate method of gauging distance, as long as you keep your stride length fairly uniform.

Dead reckoning: By knowing your average walking pace and the time you have been walking you should be able to estimate the distance travelled. The Scottish mountaineer, William Naismith, came up with a reasonably reliable estimation of walking speeds and therefore distances covered. Naismith's Rule, as it is now known, estimates that an average person walks at 5 kilometres/3 miles per hour (ignoring stops of course) but add 30 minutes for every 300 metres/1000 feet climbed. Deduct about ten minutes for every 300 metres/1000 feet you descend. If the terrain is tough going you may need to reduce the estimated walking speed.

With this estimate in mind, you should set realistic daily distances, and know how long it should take you to reach a given point.

Focus points

* Having good navigation skills can save lives and prevent disasters.
* Basic map and compass skills must be practised and perfected.
* Carry back-up maps and compasses.
* Compasses can be improvised.
* Know how to use the sun, moon and stars to find north.

Next step

Having acquired the survival essentials, you should have a better appreciation of how planning ahead and taking the right equipment can make all the difference, especially when things go wrong. It is time to start adding more specialist survival skills to your bank of life-saving techniques.

9

Ropes and knots

In this chapter you will learn:

▶ *The usefulness of rope*
▶ *How to make improvised cord*
▶ *The importance of rope care*
▶ *Some basic knots*

Ropes, and the ability to use them, can be life saving. Whether making a shelter, a raft, or securing yourself on a mountain climb, knowing a few good knots can be an enormous asset. You would not want your potentially life-saving raft to break up after the first wave, simply because of inadequate knots. Rope care, and knowledge of improvised rope-making, can give you an edge in an otherwise hopeless situation.

Improvised rope- and cord-making

By their very nature, emergencies and survival situations always arrive unannounced and test our resourcefulness and determination. While we cannot predict our future, we can anticipate our likely needs.

Remember this

You can give yourself an edge by trying to foresee possible needs and packing ropes and/or bundles of parachute cord (known as paracord), in case an accident occurs or Plan A falls away due to bad weather. Simply stow some rope or cord in a protective bag in your vehicle or at the bottom of your pack, and then forget about it. You can also substitute your bootlaces with lengths of paracord. It is amazingly strong and individual threads can easily be separated out if thinner thread is needed.

There may be times when you simply don't have enough cord, or the right type for a particular job. This need not spell disaster as cord and rope-making from plants and the materials around you is always possible.

Cord and rope can be made by plaiting thin lengths of fabric, bark, animal hide or even cut-up strips of unnecessary clothing. Depending on how necessary it is to have a length of rope, you could consider cutting up your inner tent into strips and plaiting them together. You should also consider unravelling the stitching on your kit bag on occasion. Bits of wire, rucksack straps and belts can all be used for jobs that you would usually use cord for.

Here are some useful methods of making improvised cord from two commonly found plants:

Willow bark: Willow is a very useful and relatively common tree found near water. Most of us can identify a weeping willow without reference to a field guide. Its bark is easiest to remove over the spring and summer months. Thin strips of the bark can be boiled up for 40 minutes or so and softened. This should make it pliable enough for more intricate work. The inner bark will be naturally more pliable and easy to work with. Either cut into thin strips and use them as they are, or plait several strips together for added strength.

If the willow is not available, try any tree. Remember the inner bark will be more flexible, but boiling up should soften most barks enough be able to work with them.

Stinging nettles: Nettles are very common in the northern hemisphere, and again easily identified without having to refer to a plant identification guide. Remember that the leaves are an excellent food source, being rich in iron; boil for a few minutes to remove the sting. The stems can also be used to make cord. Collect tall-stemmed examples that look old. Protect your hands from the stings if you can. Remove the leaves and flatten the stems with a rock or by rolling with a heavy stick on hard ground. Remove the pith and separate the split stem into strands; plait together to make a thin cord. You can then plait several lengths of thin cord to make thicker, stronger cord. Try to keep the thickness of each strand/plait as similar as you can, to prevent weak spots.

Vines and thin green twigs can also be used to make a twine of sorts, and perhaps be adequate for shelter making. However, you will need something stronger for raft making.

Try it now

Purely as an exercise, see if you can make yourself approximately two metres of cord from willow bark. Get to experience the work needed and techniques required **before** a situation arises that has your well-being at stake.

Basic rope care

Your ropes and lengths of cord may literally be your lifeline to safety, or at least a way out of considerable discomfort. You must look after them as your wellbeing may depend upon their continued usefulness. Here are a few basic rules:

▶ Protect against excessive sunlight, damp and dirt.

▶ Protect against possible rodent and insect ruin (e.g. by not storing on the ground or in a dark shed), as some insects and rodents will nest in a coiled rope and chew it up.

▶ Do not allow ropes to drag on the ground, and keep them clean.

▶ Seal the ends against fraying by whipping, taping, daubing with glue or melting over (if it has a high nylon content).

▶ Protect against chemicals such as petrol and methylated spirits.

▶ Never tread on a rope. Dirt gets into the fibres which, when the rope is moved and used, tear and rip the fibres apart. This ultimately weakens the rope dangerously and unnecessarily.

▶ Try to know the rope's age and manufacturer's recommendations. Climbers ought not to use old ropes for life preserving. Ropes have a recommended life, after which they cannot be relied upon and may break.

▶ Don't allow your ropes to pass over and rub against anything abrasive like a rock edge. Instead, slip an item of clothing underneath the rope as this should prevent any unnecessary wear.

▶ Learn to properly coil your ropes and cords. A mass of tangles can take a very long time to unravel and you may not always have time on your side in an emergency.

- Do not leave rope stretched and under tension any longer than is necessary.

- Do not leave rope knotted any longer than necessary.

- Inspect your ropes regularly for any signs of deterioration, nicks and wear spots. Cut out the damaged areas and re-seal the ends. If ignored, these weak spots will be where the rope breaks under load. That load may be you on a one hundred metre abseil.

Using ropes

Always be aware that certain ropes are more suited to a particular task than others. This is the beauty of paracord, in that you can pull out the inner strands for more intricate jobs, or to use as fishing line.

You should never cut a cord or rope unless you really have to. If you start cutting ropes and cord, you'll soon have handfuls of odd lengths, all with unsealed ends. The rope may be too weak or too short to do a job if you tie several pieces together. If you have too much cord for a particular task, don't cut it, simply coil round the excess and tuck it in somewhere. The next task may be more important and need every inch of cord you have.

Tie knots that can be undone easily and consider carrying a marlin spike to help undo tight knots. Many military issue folding knives have spikes on them for this purpose.

Remember this

Fingers get numb in the cold and wet, and tying or untying a secure but intricate knot may cost valuable time, or simply be impossible under certain conditions. Think ahead.

If you have to throw a rope, perhaps across a river to a mate, it will be easier if the leading end is weighted. Tie a rock or something heavy to one end and then swing it around over your head until you think you have enough power to let it go over your obstacle. If you are trying to throw a heavy rope a reasonable distance, it may be easier to hurl a rock with just a thin cord attached; then attach the thin cord to the heavier rope and pull it over.

Useful knots

Learning how to tie various knots is a practical skill that has to be acquired first hand. It is not a skill that can be learned through reading alone or even watching someone – you have to actually do it yourself. Although sailors and mountaineers become familiar with a great many knots over time, to a survivor or someone who spends a fair amount of time outdoors, learning just a few knots are all that is normally required to deal with most situations.

The type of rope or cord used, in terms of thickness and material, make them suitable (or unsuitable) for certain applications. However, in many cases you have to make do with what you've got. Your ability to adapt whatever you have to hand may prove crucial when accidents happen and a life-threatening situation unfolds before you without warning.

Here are a few knots that may prove useful.

▶ The bowline

This is a non-slip loop and is widely used by both mariners and mountaineers alike. The knot is very useful as it can be tied quickly and easily and yet is reliable and very strong. As the loop doesn't tighten under strain, it can be used in hauling injured parties off mountains, etc., as it won't tighten around them dangerously as you pull them to safety, or lower them down.

As the Figure 9.1 shows, you make a small loop, thread the end of the cord up and through the loop, take it around the longer part of the cord and then back down the loop. Pull the shorter end to tighten.

▶ Running bowline

This is a loop that will tighten under strain and so can be useful to fasten things together and to make snares if wire is not available.

To tie, simply make a bowline and then pass the long end through the loop. Nothing to it (see Figure 9.1).

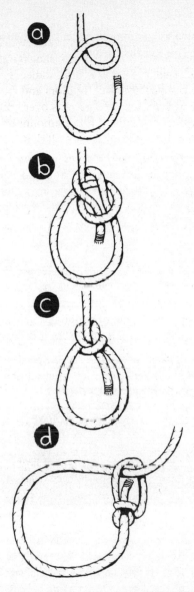

Figure 9.1 How to tie a bowline (C) and running bowline (D) (© Kate Polley)

▶ Reef knot

Sometimes known as a square knot and familiar to any Boy Scout I'm sure. This knot is used to tie two ropes together where they are of approximately the same thickness. It should not be used for nylon ropes, as it tends to slip. The reef knot is often used in bandages as the knot lies flat rather than being a raised lump, and is therefore a bit more comfortable for the injured patient.

It is easily tied by passing the right end over and under the left end, then by putting the left end over and under the right end. If you get it wrong, you'll end up with a messy looking granny knot, which is both weaker and very difficult to undo once tightened up. See Figure 9.2.

▶ Double sheet bend

This is a very useful knot that gets quite frequent use when the unexpected happens. It is used to tie two ropes together where they are of the same or different thickness, or perhaps very wet and therefore at risk of slipping. Extremely useful and something you must practise long before it is possibly needed.

As the diagram shows, the thinner cord/rope simply wraps itself around the looped thicker rope a few times and once pulled tight is reliable and strong. See Figure 9.3.

 ## Case study

In the world of travel and adventure, the survival story of Aron Ralston stands out as being one of the grittiest. So remarkable was his escape from death that it was made into a successful film, *127 Hours*, which virtually every climber and adventurer has seen, and winced through.

Ralston was an experienced climber and outdoorsman. He had decided to explore the remote desert canyons of Utah, partly by mountain bike, and partly on foot. He took very little, but did have some rope, a multi-tool, a small first aid kit, and about a litre of water. He had not told anyone where he was going.

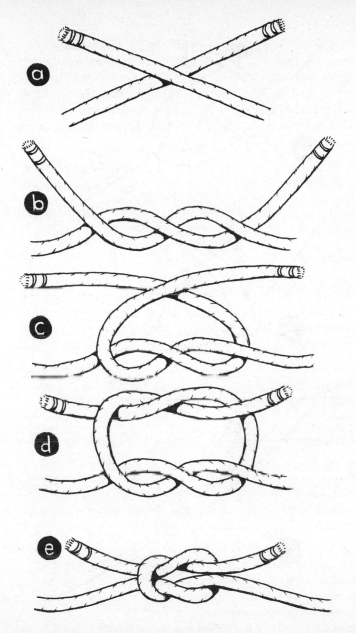

Figure 9.2 How to tie a reef knot (© Kate Polley)

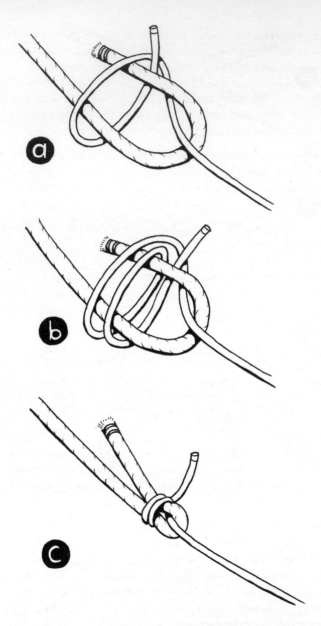

Figure 9.3 How to tie a double sheet bend (© Kate Polley)

Having parked his bike, Ralston was climbing and scrambling around the sandy ravines, canyons and old river routes when the accident happened. Many of the deep gullies had large boulders stuck on top of them, which were too large to drop down any further. These crevices had been cut into the earth after thousands of years of erosion by wind and water. Catching his breath and no doubt enjoying the view, Ralston stood on top of a huge boulder that had become wedged in a dried ravine.

The boulder moved, and slipped down further, taking Ralston with it. They both dropped down the narrow slot. Ralston was relatively unharmed, but his right arm had become pinned by the boulder and no matter how hard he tugged and twisted, he could not pull it out.

Ralston was out of sight should anyone be nearby, which was extremely unlikely. This remote part of Utah's desert had been a favourite hideout for Butch Cassidy and the Sundance Kid, and any passing traffic, be it on foot, bike or horse, was rare. Ralston realized no one would even alert the police for another day or two, and even then they would not know where to start looking. Rescue was therefore improbable. His survival was going to be down to him.

Days passed. What little water and provisions he had soon ran out. Attempts to chip away at the boulder with his multi-tool failed, as did trying to move the huge rock by force. Time was running out, and soon he would be too weak to save himself. Using the blunt blade of his multi-tool he started cutting off his trapped arm. He drifted in and out of consciousness during the process.

Although the blunt blade did eventually cut through the skin and soft tissue, Ralston could not cut or saw through the bones in the forearm. By repositioning himself as best he could, he was able to exert enough power to snap and break his bones and, with a bit more cutting, freed himself.

He made a tourniquet and reduced the blood loss. With his uninjured arm, he used the rope he had brought with him to escape the ravine. Ralston chanced upon some people taking photographs, and rescue and medical help was called in. The ordeal cost him a limb, but not his life. Ropes, cordage, tourniquets, all contributed to his escape, but there were many lessons to be learned. The full story can be found in Aron Ralston's own account in his book, *Between a Rock and a Hard Place*.

Focus points

* Rope and cord can be made by plaiting together strips of willow bark or lengths of nettle stems.

* Ropes must be cared for and stored properly – your life may depend upon their condition.

* Learning four simple knots alone will give you an advantage in a survival situation.

* Having lengths of rope and/or cord in your pack or vehicle should be considered an essential part of your outdoor equipment as their versatility and usefulness are simply too great to leave behind.

Next step

If you like spending time outdoors, one of your frequent concerns will be the weather. On boat trips, as well as hikes and mountain climbs, being able to understand, and perhaps predict, the weather ahead of you can be extremely advantageous.

Understanding the weather

In this chapter you will learn:

▶ *The usefulness of knowing the weather conditions*

▶ *How to read the sky and predict the likely weather ahead of you*

▶ *The effects of forthcoming weather on animals and plants*

▶ *The basic cloud types and what they mean*

▶ *Sources of weather forecasts*

The ability to understand and predict the weather will help in deciding when to move and when to stay put. It will also assist in choosing the right kit and clothing. While you may not be able to control the weather, knowing what lies ahead will enable you to prepare properly and stay more comfortable.

Remember this

Since you lose body heat 25 times faster when wet, avoiding rain can mean avoiding hypothermia and staying alive.

Case study

I had been travelling in China for several months, always preferring the remoter parts and getting out into the countryside whenever I could. I had managed to get some rickety local transport to a small mountain village, which was only about ten miles from a Taoist monastery I wanted to visit. I would have to continue the rest of my journey on foot, and estimated it should take about three hours.

Before I set off, I noticed the sky, the birds and the plants. There was a noticeable stillness about everything. The plants smelled stronger than normal, and the scent of the roadside flowers was particularly distinct. An easterly wind was blowing, and large clouds were merging together and getting darker. There were no birds in the sky that I could see, and the far-off ringing of bicycle bells seemed sharp and clear.

Put together, the signs signified the likelihood of rain in the very near future. I did not have an especially good waterproof coat with me, and my destination was about several hours away along a dirt track with little tree cover. It might take longer if I got lost. It was still mid-morning and I was in no hurry. I decided to act upon the signs around me, enjoy a few more cups of jasmine tea, and stay put. Within the hour, rain poured down producing lake-like puddles and impassable, mud-sliding footpaths. Locals ran for cover, while others became drenched in moments. The dark skies grew darker, and lightning began to flash and thunder boomed.

Had I ignored the signs, I would have been extremely wet and uncomfortable. In the wilderness and on the mountains, this could have escalated to hypothermia. My discomfort could have caused me to make errors of judgement, acted rashly, and I could have become lost simply through irritation and coping with the foul weather. Furthermore, because of the openness of the land, I would have exposed myself to lightning strikes.

Once the rain stopped and the clear skies returned, I set off again and arrived safely within my estimated timescale. You can choose to ignore the weather signs if you have access to dry clothes and only a short distance to travel. In all other cases, observe your surroundings: weigh up the risks of delaying your onward journey with those of being caught in bad weather.

What is 'weather'?

Weather means the current conditions of temperature, humidity, rainfall, etc. for an area. The 'climate' means the average or usual weather that has occurred over a long period of time in a particular area. Climate charts are readily available for most parts of the world and are found in foreign guidebooks or on websites such as www.weatherbase.com. If travelling abroad, or even to a different part of a large country, it is recommended that you check the expected conditions for that time of year.

There is no point planning a two-week trip during the rainy season of a tropical country if you can go at another time. Crossing deserts at the coolest time of year is usually better than going at the hottest. Your clothing, kit, choice of tent, type of transport, even water supplies, can be tailored to the expected conditions. Although weather conditions cannot be guaranteed, knowing what usually happens at the time you intend to be there will help in your planning.

Weather signs

Rain and other changes in the weather never arrive unannounced. As with many survival skills, heightening your awareness of the world around you can give you a potentially life-saving advantage. Weather forecasting is perhaps of only passing interest to those hiking (who may accept it will rain occasionally), but will be of great value to those climbing mountains or sailing in ships, and who would prefer to know about an approaching storm or blizzard.

▶ The sky

The sky is a major source of information and you should note the following:

▶ As the old rhyme reminds us, a red sky at night is indicative of the following day being fine and dry; a grey morning also indicates a fine day ahead. A red sky in the morning is a possible indicator of a wet day ahead. Not always 100 per cent accurate, but often a good indicator, especially if there are other signs indicating the same.

▶ Normally, weather moves from west to east, so if a storm is on its way, the western sky will look threatening.

▶ The bluer the sky, the greater the chance of dry, fine weather. This is because sunlight contains all the colours of the spectrum, each having a slightly different wavelength. The shortest is blue and this is obscured if the air contains too much moisture. Moisture-laden skies look white. Blue means dry, white means wet.

▶ Halos around the sun or moon are indicators of a forthcoming change in the weather. An enlarging halo means good weather is coming, whereas a shrinking or tightening halo means the reverse and the possibility of rain.

▶ Rainbows in the late afternoon are a reasonably accurate sign of good weather ahead.

▶ Clear night skies are usually followed by dry weather. It should be remembered that, as clouds act like blankets in keeping the Earth's heat in, a cloudless night will be a cold one and possibly cause frost.

▶ Early morning mist rising from a valley is a sign of good weather ahead. In hilly country, however, if the mist has not lifted by midday, it will probably remain, and possibly turn to rain.

▶ The wind

Generally, wind blowing from the west brings dry, settled weather. This doesn't apply if you are on the west coast of a continent. Similarly, a wind from the east often brings unsettled and stormy weather. These are general guidelines, so start noticing the wind and weather patterns in your area, and see how reliable they are.

Always note the prevailing wind when you are out. Winds, like tides, are pretty regular and blow in a consistent direction – trees and vegetation often indicate from what direction the wind usually blows. Winds are the result of the heat differences between certain parts of the planet, particularly the poles and the equator. The unequal heating sets up unequal pressures and this causes wind. Ancient navigators (and modern-day survivors) have used them as navigational aids for thousands of years. Many regular winds have been named, for example, the Mistral, Harmattan, Sirocco, Chinook and the Australian Brickfielder.

▶ Sound

Sounds seem clearer when wet weather is imminent. An approaching storm pushes the warm air that is usually close to the ground up and on top of a band of cold air. This causes sound waves to be bent back down to the ground, making them appear nearer and louder.

▶ Plants

The smell of vegetation is often more distinctive and noticeable shortly before the arrival of rain. This is because flowers and plants sense the forthcoming rain, and open up in readiness to receiving the life-giving water.

Some flowering plants like daisies and scarlet pimpernels open their petals when the weather is fine but close them as rain approaches. The small pimpernels are relatively common roadside plants in Britain, are often referred to as the 'poor man's barometer' so accurate are they at detecting fluctuations in pressure.

Try it now

Start noticing common flowers and pine cones, and see how they open and close with the weather.

▶ Smoke

If the smoke from your fire drifts straight up, it is a sign of fine and settled weather. If the smoke swirls and is even beaten down to the ground, it is a sign of approaching wet weather. Don't ignore the signs.

▶ Birds

Insect-eating birds can be seen high in the sky on fine days but closer to the ground before wet weather approaches. This is primarily because their food sources, insects, fly high in good weather, but stay low during wetter weather.

▶ Pressure

Atmospheric pressure alters with the weather but, usefully, changes can be observed before the actual arrival of the weather change. The specific pressure at any one time is largely irrelevant. It is the gradual change or trend that you need to note. If the pressure is dropping, rain is likely; if the pressure is climbing, fine weather is likely. Therefore if you have a barometer, note the reading every 30 minutes or so to see whether the pressure is gradually rising or falling.

Some outdoor watches (e.g. a Suunto Vector) have an built-in barometer which displays both the exact pressure reading at a given moment and, more usefully, a small graph showing the pressure trend over the last six hours. A very useful aid to keeping dry!

▶ Pain

A sudden drop in pressure, signifying the possibility of wet weather, can be detected in some sensitive people. The joints and soft tissues can become painful with a rheumatism-type discomfort which may be indicative of forthcoming rain.

▶ Clouds

There are ten main cloud types, the key differences being their shape and altitude. It is not necessary to learn their Latin names or to be able to identify them all on sight. A basic understanding of their movements and when rain might arrive is sufficiently useful:

- The higher the clouds the finer the weather, as rain falls from low clouds not high ones.

- Clouds hanging on high ground are usually a sign of rain, unless they have moved on by noon.

- Fluffy white clouds are a sign of fair weather when separated out, but once they start merging into one large tower-like cloud, rain won't be far off.

- If the wind is blowing from the east, the pressure is dropping, and low, dark clouds are forming, rain is inevitable.

- High clouds contain ice crystals and can form halos around the sun and moon. Once the clouds thicken they drop and light is obscured, no halos are formed and shadows are few. Rain is close and, as the clouds descend even further, they become darker as the pressure keeps falling. Time to get the poncho out.

Key idea

Forecasting is made more accurate by taking into account as many weather signs as you can. Do not rely on one sign alone to accurately predict the weather. As illustrated in the case study above, the more weather signs you can observe, the more accurate the prediction will be.

Extreme weather

▶ Tornadoes

These violent storms are often associated with low pressure and can generate wind speeds of up to 400 miles per hour. They are most common in the USA and Australia. They are noisy enough to be seen and heard before they are too close.

Take evasive action by moving away at right angles to its apparent path. Take cover in something solid (e.g. a cave), or underground if you can. Stay away from caravans, vehicles, and anything that could be hurled at you. If stuck in a building, get to the ground floor and keep away from the windows and rooms with large free-span ceilings in case they collapse. Protect yourself under something either cushioned or protective.

► Lightning

If thunder occurs less than 60 seconds after lightning, the lightning is very close by and precautions should be taken to avoid being struck. Find shelter avoiding high ground, open spaces or trees if you can. If caught out in the open, crouch on the ground, trying to minimize how much of your body is touching the ground. Try standing or sitting on something dry, like a coiled rope. You can seek safety in a cave as long as you go in at least three metres. In mountain areas, avoid standing under rocky overhangs as lightning can be routed through them. If in a building, stay away from the windows and avoid using land-line telephones.

Avoid holding any metal objects unless they have an insulated or wooden handle.

► Hurricanes

This means the wind has reached force 12 on the Beaufort wind scale. The combination of strong wind and torrential rain usually spells chaos and destruction. Do not attempt to travel in a hurricane and take cover in solid buildings, caves, ditches or behind large rocks. Avoid anything that could be blown your way, including windows and vehicles. Keep a radio to hand as hurricanes can be monitored via satellite, so warnings, and the all clear, will be announced on local radio stations.

Official sources

You can find out about the weather in any part of the world by clicking on to one of the following websites:

► www.ukweather.com – provides ten-day forecasts and weather information to most destinations worldwide

► www.metoffice.gov.uk – The British Meteorological Office site

► www.bbc.co.uk/weather – The BBC's official weather site

► www.cnn.com/weather – CNN's international weather information site

You cannot control the weather but, as an outdoor person, you ought to know the likely weather ahead of you and prepare accordingly. Ignorance is avoidable, and can prove extremely dangerous.

Focus points

* Knowing the likely weather ahead of you can be used to dictate your movements, your kit and your clothing.
* Pay attention to the sky and the clouds as they are great indicators of the weather.
* Flowers smell stronger just before the rain, and insect-eating birds fly lower in the sky.
* Ignoring the weather signs may mean you expose yourself to weather conditions that could affect your mental concentration and well-being.

Next step

One of the more important survival skills you need is the ability to look after yourself and others in the event of accident or illness. You have to know what medicines and first aid equipment to take on a trip, plus what can be used in the wild if you do not have exactly what you need.

11

Medicine and first aid

In this chapter you will learn:

▶ *How to obtain expert medical support*
▶ *What to include in a medical kit*
▶ *About medicinal plants for common conditions*
▶ *How to make an insect repellent in the wild*
▶ *How to deal with cuts, sprains and heart attacks*

Imagine you are miles away from proper medical assistance and you, or one of your group, falls ill or is injured. Would you know what to do? An essential part of any survival training programme is acquiring an above average medical knowledge of that can be applied in the wild. Medical knowledge forms part of an insurance policy that will keep you and your team alive if accident or illness occurs. It also extends your freedom to parts of the world where there is no medical support available, and where you will have to be very self-sufficient.

Medical concerns and preparations specific to certain areas, such as jungles or mountains, are covered in later chapters. What follows in this chapter is the basic minimum knowledge you ought to have and should be building upon.

Courses

Try it now

You must enrol on a first aid course, and attend the regular refreshers. Contact British Red Cross, your local ambulance service, or similar, for details of courses in your area. Local adult education centres also run courses – you have no excuse for remaining ignorant!

First aid courses will show you how to deal with basic physical injuries, such as fractures, cuts, burns and dislocations. They will teach you how to properly apply dressings, secure a broken arm, and how to give cardio-pulmonary resuscitation (CPR). This kind of knowledge is useful, but does not include everything an outdoor person needs to know. Accept the limitations of these courses and the associated manuals, and build upon them.

More specialist medical courses aimed at outdoor enthusiasts and travellers are also available. There are several companies and organizations that run courses aimed at people planning trips to remote places, and having to rely only on themselves for medical aid. They go way beyond the usual first aid course (which is largely concerned with keeping someone alive until an ambulance arrives) and cover a range of medical conditions.

See Appendix 4 (Taking things further) at the end of this book for their contact details.

Although larger expeditions and groups often have an accompanying doctor, medic or nurse as part of the team, it is vitally important that you teach yourself an above-average level of first aid and medical information. Try to avoid being in a position where your health is in the hands of others; their help may not be available in the wilderness or some remote corner of the globe.

Medical kits

Special pre-packed medical kits tailored to the expected needs of travellers and expeditions are on offer. Nomad Travel (www.nomadtravel.co.uk) and the Medical Advisory Services for Travellers (www.masta-travel-health.com) both have a range of excellent kits and medical accessories. Many of these medical kits come with sterile needles and scalpels. In most cases, you may still need to add a few items specific to you and your trip, but they are excellent starting points.

Remember this

It is absolutely vital that you know what each item of your medical kit is for, and how to use it.

One useful company, E-med, also operates a 24-hour online medical service (www.e-med.co.uk), which may benefit travellers when abroad and unable to obtain quality medical advice locally.

Personally, I prefer to make up my own kit, customized to my destination and anticipated circumstances. Things normally included are:

▶ Immodium, or other anti-diarrhoea drug containing loperamide

▶ Dioralyte rehydration sachets

▶ codeine phosphate – a good painkiller, which doubles up as anti-diarrhoea medication

▶ anti-histamines (the non-drowsy type, like Clarityn)

- painkiller, e.g. Ibuprofen
- eye drops, e.g. Optrex
- antiseptic cream or wipes
- anti-malarials
- antibiotics, wide spectrum type
- insect repellent, containing DEET
- water purification tablets
- anti-fungal cream, especially if off to humid climates
- thermometer
- crepe bandage, for sprains
- non-adherent dressings, e.g. Melolin
- assorted plasters
- sterile swabs
- triangular bandage and safety pins
- steristrip or butterfly wound closures
- gauze dressings
- burns dressings
- tweezers
- anti-AIDS kit – sterile needles, etc. – to pass to a doctor to use on you.
- dental kit – emergency fillings, oil of cloves.
- superglue, for emergency dental repairs, also as an emergency wound closure.

Run your list past your doctor, as some items may be prescription-only medicines. Most items however should be obtainable from a good chemist or one of the above suppliers.

I prefer to carry a small medical kit in a pocket or on my belt as part of a survival kit, and then carry a larger medical kit in my rucksack. The smaller kit contains items most commonly needed, for example to deal with blisters, headaches, sprains, etc., and is more accessible.

Bush medicine

Key idea

You should never have to rely so heavily on your medical kit that, without it, you would be lost and an illness or injury would worsen. For example, consider the properties of sugar. It is useful if you are dehydrated, as sweet drinks are better than plain water. Pouring neat sugar into a wound has been found to accelerate healing, slow down bleeding, and ward off infection. Sugar can also make foul-tasting food (and medicine) palatable. It can boost your blood-sugar if you are depleted and needing short-term energy.

Plants are often rich in medicinal properties, and can be prepared in one of the following ways:

▶ **Poultice:** mash up the plant and apply the pulp to a wound.

▶ **Decoction:** mash up the plant, soak for about 20 minutes, then boil up until a third of the liquid has boiled away. As a rough guide, use about a litre or 1–2 pints of liquid per handful of plant material.

▶ **Infusion:** crush a few leaves, or stems of the plant, add to a cup of hot water

▶ **Raw:** many plants, or parts of them such as fruits, can be eaten raw.

Here are some common ailments and cures:

Constipation: take a decoction of dandelions, using the whole plant. Alternatively drink warm water, eat plenty of fruit, or try a decoction of walnut tree bark.

Diarrhoea: stop eating for 24 hours, and then try an infusion of mint, or a decoction of elm or oak tree bark. Infusions of bramble leaves or hazel leaves also work, as do cups of very strong ordinary tea. Slowly introduce very plain, non-spicy food.

Stomach upsets: stop eating for 24 hours. Swallow small bits of charcoal or drink little pieces mixed with water to make a slurry, as charcoal absorbs poisons. A decoction of dandelions, or an infusion of mint leaves and stems will also calm the stomach. Slowly introduce very plain, non-spicy food.

Pain: try a decoction of willow bark and leaves, or an infusion of birch leaves. Mint or sage infusions will soothe a sore throat, as will gargling with warm salt water. Cooled, strong tea will relieve the pain of a burn: simply soak the dressings and apply directly to the wound.

Bleeding: apply a poultice of bruised plantain leaves. Eating green leafy vegetables such as spinach will accelerate coagulation because of the high vitamin K content.

Infection: clean the wound with water first. Natural antiseptics include infusions of thyme, lavender oil, garlic juice, onion, vinegar, and good old alcohol. Urine, which is sterile, can be used to clean wounds. Fungal infections can be dealt with by keeping the site dry and exposing to strong sunlight. Honey applied like a paste can counter infections if desperate. Peat moss absorbs nasties if placed over a wound, and will aid healing. Dock leaves and burdock root are also good antiseptics.

Earaches: drip some onion juice into the ear. Its antiseptic properties can help. Take any form of painkiller you have.

Insect repellents

Insects may not always kill you, but they can distract you and cause serious accidents by impairing your judgement. Some insects can pass on very unpleasant diseases which *can* ultimately kill you. Take them seriously. Deal with malarial mosquitoes by (a) taking the necessary daily/weekly tablets, (b) using a repellent applied to your clothing and exposed skin, and (c) sleeping under a mosquito net, or in a windy/smoky place that should keep them away.

Try using some of the following as a general insect repellent if you run out of the proper stuff:

- garlic or onion rubbed over any exposed skin

- oak bark boiled into tannin

- smoke from a fire will keep most insects at bay

- tobacco rubbed on the skin

- pepper rubbed on the skin works the same way

- mud smeared over places you can't cover up easily will give you some relief

The above are not always very practical or long-lasting, but may help. If bitten, do not scratch the bite. Something very cold, such as ice, applied to the bite will relieve the itchiness. Bee stings and ant bites are acidic, and can be neutralized by applying something alkaline, such as toothpaste. Wasp stings are alkaline and can be countered by applying something mildly acidic, such as vinegar. Always try to carefully remove the sting from the skin first.

Try it now

Carry a credit card size 'tick card' to enable you to safely remove ticks. They are common in areas where deer and sheep roam, and through which you may walk or camp. Ticks can cause infection at the bite site, but also carry disease.

Dealing with heart attacks

People push themselves, especially older people wanting to prove themselves to the younger team members, or perhaps just to themselves. For a variety of reasons, including diet, lifestyle and genetics, people have heart attacks and die in remote places, often surrounded by people who did not know what to do.

If someone collapses from a heart attack, it is often after experiencing some of the following symptoms:

- intense pain, usually in the centre of the chest which can feel like a tightness or squeezing

- pain moving from the chest to the arms (often the left arm), or to the jaw, neck, back or abdomen

- shortness of breath

- feeling sick or actually being sick

- feeling a sense of anxiety, like a panic attack

- light-headedness

If the person collapses and appears not to be breathing or moving, check for a response by shouting or slapping them. Don't worry about trying to find a pulse; it may be too weak to detect, especially if you and the casualty are cold, and if you do not regularly check for pulses. If the person does not respond, assume they have had a cardiac arrest, call for an ambulance (or send someone off to get one), and commence cardio-pulmonary resuscitation (CPR):

1   Put the person on their back. Place your hands on the centre of their chest and, with the heel of your hand, press down 5–6cm at a steady rate. Aim to go slightly faster than one compression per second.

2   After every 30 chest compressions, give two breaths. Tilt the person's head back gently and lift the chin up with two fingers. Pinch the person's nose. Seal your mouth over their mouth and blow steadily and firmly into their mouth. Check that their chest rises; give two breaths.

3   Keep up the 30 chest compressions to two breaths routine until the person either recovers or an ambulance arrives.

Dealing with wounds

The immediate treatment for cuts is to apply pressure and stop the bleeding, assuming there is nothing in the wound, like glass, pressing deeper into the skin. Smother the wound with a cloth and simply press hard until the bleeding is under control. Wash with clean water and apply antiseptic once the bleeding slows or stops.

Most of us like to close up a nasty cut, but in the wild this may mean shutting in bacteria that will breed and possibly turn into something lethal. Sometimes a better option, once bleeding has been controlled, is to leave the wound apart and open, thereby making it easier to clean thoroughly. Still cover the wound completely, but don't worry about pulling the skin together in an attempt to join the two edges. If you have any, apply lots of antibiotic/antiseptic treatments a few times a day. You may scar, but if you clean the wound frequently it will reduce the risk of blood poisoning from infection.

If closing the wound is appropriate, consider using superglue, or drawing the skin together with strong tape or purpose-made adhesive sutures. Stitching is tricky, painful, and exposes the wound to further infection. This is best left to hospital staff once you get back to safety.

Sprains

Sprains are common, especially ankles. Hikers carrying heavy packs, and climbing over stiles, fences, gates, and other obstacles, all too frequently lose their footing and twist an ankle. In the first 48 hours apply RICE – Rest, Ice around the wound, Compress with a tight crepe bandage, then Elevate. After the first 48 hours, apply CHER – Compress as before, apply Heat to speed circulation to the damaged area, Elevate, and Rest.

Water as a medicine

I knew a medic in Algeria who considered water one of his most useful 'medicines'. Many illnesses and conditions are made easier to deal with if you have pure water to hand. For example, if suffering from diarrhoea, it is important to keep your fluid intake up to prevent dehydration. Similarly, if suffering from constipation, regular drinks of *warm* water may help.

Wounds, if kept clean with sterilized water, will be less prone to infection. Burns can be treated by immersing the wound in clean cold water for several minutes.

Sore eyes, from dust or glare, can be relieved by laying a cold wet cloth over the eyes. Many fevers can be treated by rest and maintaining fluid levels.

Preventative measures are often overlooked. Wash cups, spoons and bowls, as well as food, in pure water and this will lessen the likelihood of stomach and bowel problems.

Keep yourself and your hands clean when eating, and this will reduce the spread of disease and infection to any wounds. Good hygiene standards pay off, especially if out in some remote wilderness where professional medical supplies and help may be absent.

If pure, safe water is not available, make some. As noted in Chapter 3 on water, filter the water initially to remove the larger impurities and animal life, then use water sterilizing tablets to render the water safe to drink, and to use in the treatment of illnesses and accidents. If you are without water-sterilizing tablets, boiling water for several minutes should produce bug-free water good enough to use and to drink.

Case study

The wartime story of Norwegian commando Jan Baalsrud demonstrates many elements of survival, good medical knowledge being one of the key reasons he survived.

Baalsrud was one of a small team that embarked on a dangerous mission to destroy a German air control tower in Norway. The mission was compromised when he and his team accidentally made contact with a civilian shopkeeper who had the same name as their contact, but who in fact was loyal to the enemy and betrayed them.

The team tried to escape, but their boat was destroyed and sunk. Baalsrud swam ashore in ice-cold Arctic waters; he was the only soldier to evade capture. Soaking wet and missing one boot, he escaped up into a snow gully. He evaded capture for some eight weeks, suffering from inevitable frostbite and snow blindness. His deteriorating physical condition forced him to rely on the assistance of Norwegian patriots.

It was during his time hiding out in a wooden hut that Baalsrud was forced to operate on his feet with a penknife. He had enough medical knowledge to suspect that he had blood poisoning. His feet were in an awful condition and oozing a foul-smelling pus. Baalsrud cut into his feet and drained the liquid as best he could.

Too weak and injured to walk, Baalsrud was transported by stretcher and sledge. The Norwegians worked in relays, each group taking him a certain distance to where another group would collect him, and carry him further. At one point he was left at a hand-over point on a high plateau. He lay on a stretcher in the snow for days on end, as the next group could not get to him because of bad weather and enemy patrols. While he waited, lying behind a snow wall built to shelter him, Baalsrud amputated nine of his toes to stop the spread of gangrene to his feet, an action which saved them. After surviving for nearly three weeks in the snow on the plateau, the Norwegians did eventually come and find him. To their amazement he was still alive, albeit covered in snow.

He was relayed by stretcher towards the border with Finland. Then he was put in the care of some native people of northern Scandinavian who, with reindeer, pulled him on a sled across Finland and into neutral Sweden, where he was safe at last.

He spent seven months in a Swedish hospital before being flown back to Britain. Baalsrud's medical knowledge and DIY surgery prevented blood poisoning and saved his life.

A full account of this survival story is found in *We Die Alone* by David Howarth.

Rust never sleeps

Knowledge gets rusty if you do not use it. In this case, rusty medical knowledge could prove fatal to someone in need of urgent help. You must do a basic first aid course, and follow it up with the periodic refreshers. Physical practice, as well as reading and re-reading medical manuals, is necessary to keep your skills useful and immediately to hand. If you have a medical emergency, you may not have time to dig out a book and thumb through to the correct page.

You should consider becoming a First Responder medic or volunteer with the ambulance service to keep your skills sharp.

You need to overcome the initial disgust of seeing a messy wound, otherwise shock and the sight of blood will paralyse you mentally and prevent you from applying life-saving medical assistance.

Remember this

Education may be expensive and inconvenient, but ignorance is doubly so!

Focus points

✳ Enrol on a basic first aid course.
✳ Assemble a medical kit specific to your needs.
✳ Many common plants have useful medicinal properties.
✳ Take insect bites seriously and carry a repellent.
✳ Purified water can be used to treat a range of medical conditions.

Next step

Tracking is a skill that is often overlooked and thought to be the stuff of myths, or perhaps Hollywood fiction. It is not. The skill is very real and still used by hunters and naturalists around the world today. Tracking will help you know the movements of local animals – animals you may wish to avoid, or catch for food.

12

Tracking

In this chapter you will learn:

▶ *How to make a basic tracking kit*
▶ *How to prepare for tracking*
▶ *About types of clues trackers notice*
▶ *Some common animal tracks*
▶ *How to track animals*
▶ *How to age tracks and 'sign'*

Do not make the mistake of believing that the art of tracking is a long-lost skill which was only used by hunter-gatherers. The skill and practice of tracking is alive and well and still in use around the world today. Zoologists and hunters both rely on tracking skills as a means of getting close to an animal. As a survivor thrown into an unexpected situation, tracking skills may prove useful in several ways.

Once you are able to identify and age a track, you can decide whether an animal is dangerous and close by, or harmless and several days away. You may need food and, based upon the evidence, set a trap. You may also have come across bear or big cat prints, and want to keep well away.

The tracking skills discussed in this chapter have a stranded hiker/traveller/explorer in mind, and assume you want to know what animals are in your area, and what they are doing.

A tracker's preparations

In an ideal situation, a tracker will not want to alert their quarry, so where possible wear appropriately camouflaged clothing and remain out of sight. Wear quiet rustle-free clothing, and avoid ripping open noisy Velcro pockets and openings once you are near animals of interest.

Key idea

Animals use scent far more than we do, so do not start tracking after a shower in which shampoo, toothpaste and deodorant still linger. Try not to wear recently washed clothes; the soap powder will signal your presence long before you are seen or heard.

Tracking may take hours, days or even weeks and therefore requires that you are resilient, comfortable in the outdoors and doggedly persistent. Tracking is not something you ought to rush, otherwise your impatience may result in a lost trail or wrong deduction.

A basic tracking kit might include:

- notebook and soft-leaded pencil – works better in damp conditions

- large-scale map of the area

- compass

- tape measure

- Swiss army knife with tweezers

- magnifying glass

- torch

- clear glass tumbler, to examine pellets and faeces

- binoculars, preferably 7 x 42 as they are good even in low light

- night vision aid (many animals are nocturnal)

- tracking stick, used to carefully move vegetation and not disturb the ground; also used to measure the quarry's stride

- insect repellent

- field guide to tracks and animal signs

- small first aid kit

- walkie talkie or mobile phone (if there are two or more of you)

First steps

All tracks and physical evidence left by the quarry are called 'sign', both in the singular and plural. If you want to follow a particular animal, the first sign you find is all important. If it is a footprint, a sketch or photo will be made. Its dimensions should be carefully measured and any peculiarities noted down. This will be used to positively identify your animal and disregard other prints later on, and to ensure you stay on the right trail and do not inadvertently start to follow another. For the same reason, the animal's gait or stride will be measured so that, even if prints are too faint or smudged, the tracker will still be pretty sure they are following the right animal. The length of the stride will indicate whether the animal is walking or running, or perhaps hobbling because of an injury.

This step in the process may be useful to a survivor looking for a food source, as it will keep you on the track of your quarry, perhaps already speared/injured by you. It may also help you to distinguish the passing of your recent animal from the older tracks left before.

Key idea

Being able to identify a particular track could enable you to avoid a dangerous animal.

Using a detailed map of the area, you ought to then pinpoint the first evidence of the animal you are tracking, and try to work out where it might be heading. If part of a team, you can radio your findings to others who will then race ahead and attempt to intercept the animal at the possible destination, and perhaps set a trap.

Remember this

By checking your map, and making notes, you can build up a picture of where your animal goes and why.

Case study

In 1823, a frontiersman named Hugh Glass was scouting ahead with a few others as part of a fur-trapping expedition in South Dakota, USA. He was ahead of the rest of his group, and did not notice the tracks or sign of nearby bears. Unfortunately, he stumbled upon a large female grizzly bear with two cubs. The protective mother attacked him, mauling him badly. Glass drew his knife and fought the grizzly, stabbing it repeatedly as it clawed and bit into him. Hearing his screams, two of the trappers with him soon arrived and found him lying unconscious on top of the bear in a gory mess of human and animal blood. They quickly killed the dying bear with a rifle shot, and then took the dying Glass with them back to their camp.

The expedition leader took a good look at the extent of Glass' wounds and believed that he would soon die of his horrific injuries. Concerned he would hinder the expedition's progress, he asked two trappers to stay with Glass until he died, give him a good burial, and then rejoin the group as quickly as possible. Two men stayed behind, and dug a shallow grave in readiness for Glass' inevitable death.

What happened next is unclear, but the two men decided to leave the dying man under a bear skin and some branches. The two may have feared attacks by hostile Indians, other bears, or simply became bored. Either way, they left the injured man and soon caught up with the rest of the group. They lied, and reported to the expedition leader that Glass, as expected, had eventually died.

However, Glass was tougher than they realized and he did not die. He eventually regained consciousness, and woke up in his shallow grave under a thin covering of dirt and leaves. His gun and knife, outdoor clothing and other equipment, had been taken by the two men who were meant to have stayed with him.

He assessed his injuries. His leg was broken and his cuts extensive and in need of attention. The bear had cut him so badly it exposed rib bones on his back. He had lost a lot of blood, and his wounds were now infected and festering. He was alone and without proper equipment to travel or to fend for himself; he was more than 200 miles away from the nearest settlement at Fort Kiowa.

He managed to set his own broken leg, and wrapped himself in the bear hide that had covered him in the shallow grave. Not one to give in, Glass started crawling.

It took him six weeks of crawling on his hands and knees to reach the Cheyenne River, some hundred miles away from his grave site. The grizzly bear had nearly torn off part of his scalp, and he suffered from fever and advanced stages of infection. To prevent gangrene from progressing in his wounds, and possibly dying of blood poisoning, he lay on rotting logs and let maggots climb on to him and eat his dead flesh away. He was still too weak to hunt or fish, so had to survive mostly on wild berries, roots and other edible plants he found along the way. On one occasion he was able to scare a couple of wolves away from a bison they had killed, and stole some of the bison's raw meat for himself. These scraps of food kept him alive.

When he finally reached the Cheyenne River, he built a rough raft from a large fallen tree and floated down the river. Downstream he encountered a friendly Sioux Indian who fed him and tended his wounds. Eventually he succeeded in floating on his dead tree raft all the way to Fort Kiowa, and to safety.

Glass later admitted that his sole motivation to survive was revenge for being abandoned when he most needed help. After making a full recovery, he tracked down those he held responsible for his ordeal, and went on to further adventures.

Bruce Bradley's biography, simply entitled *Hugh Glass*, provides a full and fascinating account of this unusual man, who became something of a legend among the trappers and Indians of his day.

Powers of deduction

Key idea

In tracking, it will help if you know as much about your animal as possible.

Get to know your animal's feeding habits, the type of burrow it uses, the type of footprints it leaves, and what its faeces look like. Try to build up a picture or profile of your animal, and understand where it is going and why. Everything the animal leaves behind says something about it, be it a partly-eaten apple core, faeces, a nibbled leaf, or fur brushed off on a tree or caught on a fence. The frequency of the animal's stops should be noted and inferences drawn. If it is alone, work out why. If it is an animal capable of attacking you, do you think it is hungry, or well fed? When are the animal's young usually born, and are they in evidence? Try to get inside the mind of your quarry, and anticipate and predict its movements.

Sign

Sign falls into two categories, **top sign** – above ankle height, and **ground sign** – below ankle height.

The main types of ground sign include:

▸ **Faeces:** The tracker will study faeces carefully, perhaps putting it into a glass of water, letting it carefully break up, and seeing what it is made of. It will give a good indication of the animal's diet. Indications of its health may also be speculated on as watery diarrhoea will perhaps suggest poor health which may be slowing the animal down. If there is no evidence in the faeces of the kinds of food the animal usually eats, ask yourself why. Is it too sick or injured to hunt?

▸ **Food:** If partly eaten food is discarded, it may provide positive evidence of the animal having been disturbed, which offers you the opportunity to estimate when it was in the vicinity. The level of decomposition of the food, and the extent to which it has dried out or attracted insects, will assist you in narrowing down the period when it was discarded and so when the animal was at a particular point. It will also add to your knowledge of the animal's movements and habits, perhaps allowing you to anticipate where it is heading, and how far it is from your present location.

▸ **Footprints:** These are obviously easier to find on damp ground and very difficult to see on hard, stony ground. Snow and wet sand are excellent surfaces to note tracks, as are river banks and watering points where the surrounding ground is muddy and impressionable. Footprints, and the distance between them, should be measured to ensure the quarry is not confused with prints from other animals. Notice everything.

Try it now

Go to a nearby river or stream, and see if there are any footprints along the sandy or muddy bank, often on the area easiest to get down to.

CANINE   FELINE   BEAR

Figure 12.1 Animal tracks (© Kate Polley)

▶ **Disturbances:** A good tracker will notice the out of place, for example, disturbed dew across grass, trails through fields, and faint paths around large rocks and immovable obstacles. Dislodged sticks and stones in the ground will be noted too. The damp undersides of rocks and sticks may be flipped over in passing, and a sharp tracker will note the differently coloured undersides when compared to the uniformly coloured surrounding and undisturbed material. Scuffed tree roots, bruised plants and flowers, etc., should all be noticed. Work out where your animal prefers to walk, and walk on the opposite side of the path to ensure you are not at risk of covering over its prints before you have seen them.

The main types of top sign are:

▶ damaged cobwebs

▶ bent-back branches/bushes

▶ scuffs on fences, trees, stiles, rock surfaces

▶ snagged bits of fur on fences, plants, trees

▶ scared birds suddenly taking flight

Unless the animal you are tracking has wings, it *will* leave sign. Rain obviously ruins much of a quarry's sign for a tracker, which is why you should learn to move fast, and take advantage of dry, clement weather before conditions deteriorate, and rain or darkness hide your animal's tracks and sign.

LOST TRAILS

If you lose your animal's trail, there are two main means of re-finding it. One is to initially 'cut for sign'. This means starting from the last positively identified sign, and then working out in a slowly increasing circle, looking for the overlooked sign. Using the tracking stick and knowing the length of the quarry's usual stride, you should be able to estimate where the footprint/sign should be and recheck the area very closely.

Another means of finding sign is to check for any forced points of passage. These are areas where a quarry is naturally diverted and forced to pass through, e.g. natural boundaries, gaps in or under fences, and spaces between obstacles. There are also 'roads' that animals use, which allow speedier travel and have fewer obstructions: notice them. Humans travel on pathways for the same reason. Rivers often have obvious easier/safer crossing points. All these forced points of passage will be noticed by a tracker and subjected to scrutiny. Many will yield sign.

AGEING OF SIGN

With experience, a tracker will be able to estimate the age of any sign he finds. Very fresh prints are obviously a lot clearer and have sharper edges than old ones: the tracker will be able to estimate the time difference within a few hours.

The rate of browning of bruised and damaged plants will also be estimated as will the rate of decomposition of discarded or partly eaten food, as well as the animal's faeces.

The weather, past and present, will also help the tracker tie the sign to a time period. If it stopped raining four hours ago and a print is found full of water, the quarry obviously passed at least four hours ago. Simple reasoning would apply if the footprint had been dry – indicating it was made within the last four hours.

Try it now

Put a broken green twig on the ground, beside a recently-eaten apple core, or piece of orange peel. Note the time and the general appearance of the fruit, and come back in an hour. Repeat two hours later, four hours later and then, maybe, 24 hours later. Notice the effects of time; it will help you age sign in the wild. Do the same with a footprint.

Being able to age sign is a key aspect of tracking. To someone in a survival situation who is looking for a food source, there is little point in pursuing a footprint that may be a few weeks old. Similarly, not realizing a wolf print is an hour old, could be equally disastrous.

Focus points

* Tracking is a skill that helps you to hunt and avoid dangerous animals that may be close by.
* Putting together a basic tracking kit will help you.
* Know as much as possible about the animal(s) you are following: what its prints and faeces look like, life-cycle, feeding habits, and where it sleeps, etc.
* Lost trails can be found by cutting for sign or by noticing forced points of passage.
* Ageing sign is essential, and is a skill that is acquired through practice.

Next step

At some point you will have to cross a river, and there will be no nearby bridge or shallow crossing point. A raft could offer you escape from a dense jungle, far quicker than hiking could. It is now time to look at river crossing and raft making, as these two related skills can make rivers an asset in survival situations.

River crossings and raft building

In this chapter you will learn:

- ► *How to assess a river before attempting to cross it*
- ► *How to safely cross a river alone or with others*
- ► *The benefits of using a raft to travel down a river*
- ► *How to make a raft*
- ► *How to escape from a swamp or quicksand*

You cannot limit yourself to only going where there are paths and bridges. To be able to penetrate wild country and survive unexpected changes to your plans, you have to be comfortable with crossing rivers. Rafts have the potential to save you time and energy and so are worthy of consideration in many situations.

Assess the river

Remember this

Before attempting to cross a river, stand back and assess it.

You should carefully consider the following factors before getting in the water:

▶ **Location:** can you get down to the river easily? More importantly, assess where you will be able to climb up on the other side. Is it full of brambles, a steep river bank or thick mud? Plan ahead.

▶ **Current:** test the current by throwing in a stick and see where it ends up and how fast it travels. The current is fastest in the middle and on the outside edge of a bend. Ideally, you want a slow current that enables you to wade across without getting any wetter than you need to.

▶ **Hazards:** look for rocks, overhanging branches but also waterfalls and whirlpools. Walk downstream a hundred metres or so to see what lies ahead, *before* attempting a crossing.

▶ **Depth:** try to estimate the depth, which is usually deepest in the middle. Rivers are often shallow near the edge and then drop off suddenly. Be prepared and have a floatation aid to hand if you can. Carry a long stick, and gingerly prod the ground ahead of you as you cross.

▶ **Temperature:** you lose body heat around 25 times faster if wet, so you do not want to get any wetter than you have to. Hypothermia may be difficult to reverse after a long cold swim, more so if you have no means of warming yourself up afterwards. If the risk is too great, consider building a raft or crossing at another time and/or place.

▶ **Animals and fish:** in some parts of the world, you must consider whether any bankside animals or river life pose a threat. Are there alligators or piranha here? Are electric eels or catfish a problem this time of year? Do your research and know the area before you get there. If the risk cannot be avoided and you have to cross the river, know how to deal with the threatening animal or fish.

Prepare to cross

Having assessed the river and decided that crossing it is going to be necessary and manageable, there are a few other preparations you ought to make before stepping in.

When you get to the other side you are going to be cold. Anticipate this and make preparations to speed up your rewarming. Hypothermia happens when the body is no longer able to warm itself up after getting cold. Fatigue and hunger contribute to this potentially fatal condition: take it seriously. Have warm, dry clothes sealed up and ready to change into. Perhaps make up a flask before you cross. Have fire lighting stuff in a waterproof container close to hand for when you get out. Death by hypothermia can occur if you fail to plan ahead and to rewarm yourself. When you get out on the other side, you may well be very cold, and not have too much dexterity in your hands. With this in mind, do not have dry clothes or your fire starter materials in small knotted bags that shivering hands will struggle to undo.

If you have chosen to wade across, slip one arm out of your backpack and unclip the pack's waistband. If you stumble and fall, your pack could quickly fill up with water in seconds. Since a litre of water weighs a kilo, it will take only moments to be dragged down, taking you with it. You need to be able to ditch the backpack quickly if this happens, or you may risk drowning. Transfer any vital pieces of equipment, e.g. a knife, compass, matches, out of your backpack and into your pockets. Prepare for the worst case in which you lose the backpack altogether.

Wear boots/trainers for grip and protection while in the river; you do not want to risk cutting your foot on something while crossing. An injured foot will slow you down, and you may not have the luxury of time. It may also become infected, and your progress and well-being will be jeopardized.

Bag up as much clothing as you can. Clothes can take hours to dry but a wet body will take only a few minutes. Get into the river naked if need be, quickly cross, and when you get to the other side, jump around for a few moments. Do some heat-generating exercises, then dry yourself off as best you can, and put on your dry clothes.

Crossing alone

Unless you make a raft, you have to either swim or wade.

Key idea

Wading is made easier by cutting yourself a stout pole as a 'third leg'. With three points of contact on the riverbed you are less likely to lose your balance. Face upstream and carefully move across, trying to keep your legs wide apart to maximize stability. Use the pole to probe for obstacles and gauge the river's depth. Always have two points of contact with the riverbed as you move.

Swimming across a river is dangerous. The current and the cold are killers. Make a floatation aid from a kit bag, a log, or perhaps wrapping up a small bush or a bundle of twigs in your waterproof poncho. Taking cold baths before the trip will lessen the discomfort of having to swim in cold water and is worth considering if there is the expectation of having to cross rivers beforehand.

Remember this

Swimming in cold water is energy sapping and may also cause cramps. Do not jump in – the effects of shock will be worsened and, in an extreme case, you risk heart failure.

Crossing in a group

It may be safer and quicker sometimes if you all cross at once. One way is to form a rugby scrum-type position and gently wade across, each supporting one other. With numerous legs on the riverbed, anyone slipping will have immediate support.

Another way is to line up behind someone holding a support pole, as when crossing alone. You all face upstream and slowly move sideways, gripping tightly onto the waist of the person in front of you.

If you have a long enough rope, this can be used in several ways. If there are only two of you, the first person tries to cross with the rope tied around their waist, while the other holds the rope, and pulls them back if they get into trouble. The second person then tries to cross to the other side, with the other now able to pull them to safety if needed.

If there are more than two of you, a long rope can be used differently. The rope (or joined-together ropes) is made into a large loop and yet still left long enough to reach the other side. It works like this:

1 One person secures the rope to themselves and wades or swims across. Those remaining on the bank hold the rope, standing as far apart from each other as the rope will allow. If the person crossing gets into trouble, the others can haul them back.

2 Once one person is over, one of the others now secures the rope to themselves and comes over. There is now a person holding the rope on either side of the river, with one in the water pulling themselves across by holding onto the rope. Apart from the last person, all other team members follow in the same way.

3 With everyone over, the last person now ties the rope to themselves and comes over. Two others stand ready to pull them over if they get into trouble, much like in stage 1 above.

Although not all hikers will have a rope of this length, mountaineers on a trek might. Learn to use whatever you have, perhaps not always for the purpose originally intended. You could make a safety line by tying many boot laces together, perhaps tied to what rope/cord you can find, or even to a long thin branch to increase the overall length.

Remember this

You may be able to reduce or remove a risk with ingenuity and the ability to improvise.

Making a raft

If crossing a river by wading or swimming is not feasible, a raft may be the answer. A raft has several other advantages too, and is often well worth the effort for the following reasons:

▶ It enables you to travel faster, particularly in jungle areas.

▶ It allows you to travel if weak or injured.

▶ It enables you to carry heavy or cumbersome equipment through difficult terrain.

▶ It enables you to carry wounded mates more comfortably than on a stretcher.

▶ If well built, it will keep you dry and away from possibly dangerous fish and animals.

▶ It can be used as a floating platform upon which can be built a smoky fire for signalling purposes. If trying to attract rescuers, you may find there are insufficient clearings and that smoke is absorbed into the forest canopy before any spotter planes or helicopters see it.

▶ You require fewer calories per mile if travelling by river raft than if travelling on foot.

▶ As you learned in shelter making, conserve calories and use fallen trees, oil drums and any other floatable objects around you. Do not start cutting live trees and branches unless you really have to.

Here are two useful designs to consider:

▶ Log raft

Place two pliable branches on the ground, one at either end of your raft-to-be. Lay the main logs/branches on top of them. Place two more strong pliable branches on top of the logs and directly above the other two pliable branches underneath. Bend the ends of the pliable branches together, so the bottom ones get tied to the top ones, clasping the logs in between, and tie firmly. This is a quick raft to assemble and does not require much cord. See Figure 13.1.

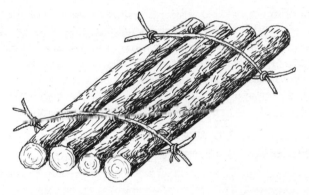

Figure 13.1 A simple raft (© Kate Polley)

Try it now

As a bit of fun, make a raft as described above. Become familiar with the kind of branches and fallen wood that are commonly available, and which are easiest to work with. Understand the physical and mental demands. Practise tying the various bits of wood and logs together. Float your raft and see how it feels to ride downstream. You do not want to make the first time you build a raft to be during a life-or-death situation, especially if you are injured or exhausted. Practising in safe conditions will make life in a survival situation much more bearable.

▶ Bamboo raft

Cut and lash together a mat of bamboo poles. The base ought to be two or three layers thick, otherwise it will not give you enough buoyancy. Secure the lengths with vine or string. If cord is short, you can skewer the poles together by making holes in the ends and driving strong sticks through.

Remember this

Tie all equipment to your raft, as it will easily fall off. It is not normally a good idea to have anything trailing behind you in case it snags on something. It is also advisable that you tie yourself to the raft in order to avoid falling off because of turbulence or fatigue.

If your raft is more than a simple floatation aid, you ought to consider making a paddle, perhaps no more than a long pole to guide and propel yourself in flat water. It is also useful to have a means of stopping yourself. Rather than carry a heavy weight, you could consider tying a bucket-like object to a rope; throw it behind you and the raft will slow down as the bucket fills up. Carry the raft around hazards, don't tackle white water.

Case study

Joe Kane's story of his near-death experience in the Amazon is significant. It shows how easily a planned trip, with the right equipment and some local help, can gradually turn into something grim and life threatening, like slowly being crushed to death by a python, and not realizing it until there is no escape.

Kane was a journalist, investigating the Huaorani Indians in Ecuador. He and his interpreter met up with the Indians, who were said to have killed outsiders in the past, and lived as primitive hunter-gatherers. Although they did not kill Kane, they did take all but a small quantity of his food supplies.

With a local guide, and inadequate food now, they moved on. They had a couple of children tag along with him. However, the local guide became alarmed at the sight of a large snake, possibly an anaconda. He abandoned Kane and his interpreter, believing the snake to be an omen, and a sign not to continue.

Kane and his small group walked for several days, during which time he injured his feet, making progress very slow and painful. The small quantity of food was now gone, and the gun Kane brought with him had no ammunition, so was useless as a hunting tool. They did, however, manage to catch and eat a small turtle, but this was still too little. Kane felt himself slowly starving to death. Soon fatigue would prevent them from continuing. Death could be the result of a silly error of judgement, an animal attack (there were no shortage of snakes, spiders, piranha, as well as jaguar), or simply not having the strength to walk on and drifting into a never-ending sleep.

The interpreter told Kane that the children still tagging along with them did not know where they were either, and that they were truly lost. They reached a river, and although they did not know which one it was, decided their survival lay in going downstream. They were in no shape to continue walking through the dense, demanding jungle. They made a raft by lashing together some tree trunks, and using vines. Paddles were simple large sapling sticks. The raft, although basic, enabled them to travel downstream. The desperate travellers sat waist deep in water as their raft carried them through the jungle. They conserved calories, and made much more progress than walking, especially as Kane's feet were in a poor state.

Their crude raft did not keep them out of the water. Travelling in the water did expose them to attack by dangerous fish, alligators and river snakes, but the risk paid off and they survived. Two days later they found help and lived to tell the tale. You can read more about Joe Kane's Amazon adventures in his two books, *Running the Amazon* and *Savages*.

Swamps and quicksand

If you stumble into a swamp or patch of quicksand, you risk an unpleasant death if you cannot get out. Move quickly, and you will accelerate your descent – and your death. Real quicksand will not necessarily pull you all the way under, but may prove extremely difficult to escape from. Instead, move slowly and you will sink slower and be able to move more easily. Try to spread your arms and legs as far apart as you can manage, and get onto your back. Use slow movements with your arms to propel yourself onto more solid ground. Panic, and you will remain stuck. As quicksand often occurs near the sea, getting stuck can means death by drowning, when the tide comes in.

Focus points

- Fully assess the risks on a crossing point before trying to cross it.
- Use a stout branch as a support when crossing, and face upstream.
- If in a group, know the various safe options when crossing.
- Rafts offer a fast and calorie-saving method of travel through jungles.
- Tie yourself and any essential equipment to the raft.
- Move very slowly to escape from quicksand. Spread your arms and legs, and roll onto your back if you sink to waist depth.

Next step

Now that you have acquired the basic skills, as well as some more specialist survival skills, you need to see how they can be applied. The next phase of your survival training concerns survival in transit: by land, sea and air. You also need to be able to deal with animal attacks, dangerous mammals, fish, reptiles and insects.

14

Travelling by land

In this chapter you will learn:

▶ *How to choose boots and clothing*
▶ *Which types of backpacks to consider and how to pack*
▶ *Route planning*
▶ *About foot care, and how to deal with blisters*

Whether on a planned trip and carrying a heavy pack across rough terrain, or having to do an unexpected trek with virtually nothing, there are certain tips and preparations you should take on board to ensure your well-being and safe arrival. Travelling by land, which usually means on foot, is what often gets us out of trouble when things go wrong, but is also what probably got us into trouble in the first place.

Boots

Key idea

Wear boots that can cope with unforeseen changes in the environment and the weather.

Well-made leather boots are usually tougher and more versatile than the lighter boots made of breathable material. These lighter boots have limitations and are better suited to situations where a change to your environment and circumstances is extremely unlikely.

Feet swell up when they get hot so buy a boot large enough to still be comfortable after hours of walking. If you shop for boots at the end of the day, when you have been on your feet for several hours, you will probably get a better-fitting boot. You do not want the boot to be so close fitting that you cannot wear thick socks (perhaps two pairs) in cold conditions.

You will get fewer blisters if your boots are shaped to your feet and there is less rubbing, so wear them as often as possible to 'break them in'. Soften the leather with either dubbin or saddle soap. Some travellers shape their boots by soaking them in water and then wearing them until they are dry.

Remember this

Keep your boots waterproofed and take extra waterproofing wax with you. Dry boots out slowly, never too close to a fire or direct source of high heat, otherwise they may crack as they dry.

Although they're a bit warm, I find shock-absorbing inner soles (e.g. Sorbothanes) excellent. Always take spare laces and some shoe glue. Life happens, and repairs may be needed while on a hike. You may need to do running repairs to enable you to reach your destination within an acceptable time frame – and before conditions turn against you or supplies run out.

Foot care

Wear socks that minimize the chances of getting blisters. A common practice is to wear a thin fine-meshed inner pair, then a thicker loop-stitched wool/nylon mix outer sock. Many camping shops sell winter and summer socks.

While waterproof socks stop water getting in, they often prevent or slow down sweat and heat getting out, and can be uncomfortable for those on the move. Gaiters can be better at keeping feet dry and protected – and they are much cooler.

Remember this

Wash your feet and change your socks daily. Use an antifungal powder with each change. Hot, sweaty feet are susceptible to various types of fungal infections that could slow you down, distract you from your task, or even stop you.

Clothing

Being on the move is usually a hot business. Unfortunately you risk freezing in sweat-drenched clothes when you stop. The layering principle will help.

1 The inner layer should be a thermal vest, a Helly Hansen 'Lifa' top for example. This draws sweat away from the skin but still keeps you warm.

2 The next layer should be a collared, long-sleeved shirt, perhaps a zipped polo neck shirt.

3 The next layer should be a fleece or woollen jumper.

4 The final layer should be a wind and waterproof jacket, and over-trousers.

Layering enables air to be trapped which is better at keeping you warm than wearing one thick layer. Long-johns and over-trousers can often be too warm to wear on the move, but are useful in very cold conditions or when you stop.

Always bring a hat and scarf as your head and neck are major sources of heat loss and need to be covered up when it gets cold, or when you stop and start to cool down.

Remember this

You must be prepared to adjust your clothing as you heat up and cool down. It might appear to be a hassle but dehydration (through excessive sweating) and hypothermia will be more so. Apathy kills! It is easier to regulate your temperature with zippered or buttoned clothing than with smocks and jumpers.

Case study

While hiking in Bolivia, I came across Dan, an American who had been there a month or so already, and had just completed a long hike in the area I was heading to. He looked a mess. He had hiked in a pair of tough, 'all-terrain' sandals, not boots. He said they proved to be ideal to start with, cool and comfortable. However, after a few days of rocky paths, marshes, and steep terrain, his feet soon became cut, heavily blistered and seemed permanently cold and wet from the boggy ground he had ended up in unexpectedly. They had the signs of very unpleasant infection where he had not been able to wash them properly or protect them.

He had worn shorts as the weather was warm when he set off, and anything thing else seemed unnecessary. However, by the end of his hike, his lower legs had become scratched by thorny bushes and rocks he had scrabbled up. They also showed the marks of dozens of bites from various insects. These too looked infected, as many bite sites were red and swollen.

To keep the weight of his backpack down, presumably to allow him to travel faster, he had taken very little clothing, no medical kit, and only the smallest amount of food. Persistent headaches, probably from a lack of food and/or water, affected his judgement, and he became lost. His anticipated short three-day hike had become five, and he had not prepared for this. Fortunately before things became any more serious, he stumbled upon a dirt track that appeared to be in frequent use. After only a few more hours of painful walking, a pick-up truck came along, and he persuaded them to take him back into town.

The lessons to be learned here are, hopefully, obvious to you by now, but for every well prepared person, there are dozens of Dans out there – all accidents waiting to happen!

Backpacks

Your pack needs to be big enough so that you do not need to tie kit to the external straps. For travellers, tying clothes and kit to the outside increases the risk of theft. For backpackers, it exposes kit to the weather and to potential loss if not securely fastened.

Backpack sizes are measured in litres. A smallish day bag is around 25 litres; a good size camping/travelling backpack is around 60 to 80 litres. Try not to fill your backpack just because you have the space. Packs with external pockets are useful to hikers; they are a good place to store a medical kit, some food, a waterproof, and anything that may need to be accessed quickly and easily. For travellers, external pockets expose you to theft as they are usually single-zipped and cannot be locked.

Most packs nowadays have an internal frame and thick waist belt. This makes them very comfortable but often quite hot. The waist belt prevents you carrying anything on your trouser belt, and this is a nuisance at times. The old external frames are cooler but more uncomfortable.

Travellers will do better with a multi-purpose pack that allows the straps and belt to be zipped away, which enables them to be carried easily on and off public transport.

Lastly, don't buy anything too cheap. The price of a backpack is determined by its size, but also by the kind of material used in its manufacture. Having a shoulder-strap tear off, or a pack split apart is no fun. Carry strong thread and a needle in case repairs are necessary.

LOADING AND CARRYING YOUR PACK

Observing some tried and tested guidelines will help:

▶ Carry no more than about a quarter of your body weight. This is not always possible, but a guideline to observe if you can.

▶ To avoid knee, ankle and back injuries, do not run while carrying your pack, especially on uneven ground. Be very careful climbing over obstacles and don't take your pack on and off during rest stops. Instead, support it on a fence or rock. Sudden movements while carrying a heavy pack can cause life-threatening injuries if you are in a remote area.

▶ Keep the pack as high on your back as possible by keeping the waist belt tight, but do not over-tighten the shoulder-straps in case you restrict the blood flow to your arms.

▶ Try to keep the heavier items of kit at the top of your pack – it will be much more comfortable to carry.

▶ Ensure your back rests against soft items of kit and not the hard edges of anything. Pack items with this in mind.

▶ Pack to make finding items easy, especially in the dark. Keep essentials either in side pockets or on the top. Put things in coloured bags, for example, your wash kit and towel in a red bag, spare clothes in a blue one. It will make finding things, especially when tired, so much easier.

▶ No pack is 100 per cent waterproof, so keep everything in a plastic bag (strong bin/garden refuse bag). This is especially important during river crossings.

Remember this

Have a survival kit, a small medical kit, some food and perhaps a radio/mobile phone in a jacket or trouser pocket, and separate from your pack. Disasters and emergencies happen and sometimes a pack is lost or has to be dumped. You may not always be able to go back and retrieve it. Don't leave yourself with nothing.

Travellers must ensure their pack can be locked in some way, perhaps by padlocking the zips together. Always keep travel documents, medicines and money on you and not in your backpack.

To keep the weight down, multi-functional kit is best. For example, ponchos can be tents, ground sheets or capes. Supplement your food, water, shelter and stove fuel with anything that can be gathered on the way. Resourcefulness and good outdoor skills will enable you to travel light.

Food is fuel

You need approximately 3,500 calories per day if on the move with a reasonably heavy pack, and more if in cold conditions. The best sources of energy are foods with a high proportion of fat or carbohydrates. Don't worry about a well-balanced, vitamin-rich diet in the short term.

Biscuits, bread, rice, pasta, potatoes, fruit, cereal bars, etc., are excellent choices of fuel – pack and eat plenty. Too few calories will make you slow, tired and accident prone.

Water loss through sweat and evaporation can be excessive and thirst is no indicator of your fluid needs. Sweetened drinks are preferable if you have a choice. As with insufficient food, dehydration will cause you to slow down, become fatigued, irritable and will lead to accidents. Watch your urine, as the darker it gets the more dehydrated you are. Inadequate fluids will also make you more susceptible to frostbite, or thrombosis if you are stuck on a hard coach seat for hours. Have water-bottles to hand at all times, and not buried away in your backpack.

Travellers should take into account the availability of toilet facilities as well as the likelihood of contaminated foods bought from street vendors. While on the move it may be safer and easier to eat foods that do not need to be cooked, like breads, nuts and biscuits. High-caffeine drinks, or supplements such as Pro-Plus, may be useful when falling asleep exposes you to theft or danger.

On the move

Plan your route, taking account of:

▶ The terrain – check the contours, marshes, wide rivers, etc.

▶ A realistic daily mileage, plus a contingency plan if your destination is unachievable. Always have a Plan B.

▶ Food and water resupply.

▶ Campsite/accommodation opportunities.

▶ Daylight hours available. Know the time the sun sets and rises. Ensure you stop with plenty of daylight time to cook, erect your tent and tend to any injuries or repairs. You do not want to be hiking in the dark, or trying to put up a tent and cooking once the sun has set.

Zigzag when going up or down steep slopes as this will put less strain on your joints and muscles. Be very careful walking over uneven ground; ankles and knees are particularly vulnerable to sprains. Carry crepe bandages, chemical ice-packs and painkillers. Keep your maps protected from the wet and any damage. Have your compass, and some food and water to hand, not deep within your pack.

If you have to travel at night, remember to allow 40 minutes for your eyes to adjust to the dark. Bilberries or blueberries, either eaten raw or in tablet form (chemists/health food shops stock them), will noticeably improve your night vision. Use red filters on any torches but if you do have to look at white light, keep one eye closed so that you can retain at least some night vision.

Case study

Juliane Koepcke's story of survival illustrates the point that being able to walk to safety is sometimes your only option. Although conserving calories and waiting for rescue might be the correct course of action in some cases, there are times when you have to make the decision to move on.

Juliane Koepcke was just 17 when the light plane carrying her and 91 others over Peru's jungle was struck by lightning and crashed. Although she probably did not realize it at the time, she was the only survivor. She was travelling with her mother, and they were on a short internal flight to see Juliane's father, who was working at a research station studying jungle wildlife.

Juliane's injuries were relatively minor considering the nature of the accident; she had a broken collar bone, a wounded arm, a swollen eye and various cuts and bruises. The mass of trees and plants had cushioned her fall to a large extent. She was not wearing any suitable clothing or footwear.

She eventually found dead bodies around her. Search planes came and went without noticing her, and she was unable to signal to them. She realized her survival lay in moving on rather than staying where she was. Despite her injuries, she *had* to walk on to survive. Flies laid eggs in her wounds, and soon hatched into maggots. With no food, and drinking river water, she continued walking.

Juliane knew that small streams usually flow into bigger ones, and ultimately into rivers. Settlements and people are usually found on the riverbanks of larger rivers. With this knowledge in mind, Juliane walked on downstream. Ten days after the plane crash, and having avoided a range of hazardous wildlife, she found a hut. While sheltering, local lumberjacks returned to the hut and found her. They attended to her wounds as best they could, and took her to safety.

Dealing with blisters

Blisters are caused by heat; rubbing causes heat, and rubbing is caused by abrasive socks and slightly loose-fitting boots. Reduce the rubbing and you will have fewer blisters. Here are a few tips to help deal with them:

▶ Attend to blisters *immediately* before they enlarge and become crippling.

▶ Where possible, cover them to prevent further rubbing and change your footwear. Bursting them exposes you to infection.

▶ However, in many cases the most practical option, if you need to continue walking, is to burst them. Pierce them with a sterilized pin/knife and then dab with antiseptic. Make a small incision and drain out the fluid. Plaster over and keep clean. Check frequently.

Before any blisters form, you should do all you can to prevent them occurring in the first place. Consider trying the following:

▶ Dab likely blister sites (or wash the feet entirely) with methylated or surgical spirits as this hardens the skin.

▶ Smear with petroleum jelly (Vaseline) to reduce friction. I have even heard of people soaking their socks in olive oil to counter friction heat.

▶ Cut toenails straight across and make sure they do not grow too long. In-grown toenails and bleeding under the nails can result if nails are either too short, or too long.

▶ Consider wearing two pairs of socks. The inner pair next to the skin should be very fine meshed, almost like a stocking. The outer pair can be heavier and rougher. This will reduce the abrasive rubbing on the skin, and help reduce blisters in the first place. Many outdoor shops sell supposedly blister-free socks that are worth trying out.

Try it now

Check the condition of your feet. Are the nails properly cut? Pack nail scissors, plenty of plasters and a tube of antiseptic cream.

Focus points

* Tough waterproof leather boots are adaptable to most conditions.
* Keep your boots waterproof by applying dubbin, or something similar, at regular intervals.
* Wear clothes in layers, not just one or two thick items.
* Pack your rucksack with weight distribution and access to key items in mind.
* Plan your route taking into account geographical features, but always have a Plan B.
* Carry a medical kit and deal with blisters early on, before they enlarge and become crippling.

Next step

Although travel by land is probably the most common for outdoors people, you need to know how to survive if you travel by boat. Whether it be a canoe, or a large ferry, boats sink and people do die. The more aware you are of the risks, and the better your preparations, the greater your chances of survival.

Travelling by sea

In this chapter you will learn:

▶ *Preparations you need to make to increase your chance of survival if the ship goes down*
▶ *What to put into a survival kit if you have to abandon ship*
▶ *How to stay alive in the sea*
▶ *How to identify signs of land being near by*

We all travel by ship or ferry at some time in our lives. Despite hi-tech navigational aids and state of the art safety features, ships still go down and passengers are still plunged into icy seas unexpectedly. While the crew may have some idea of how to survive, what about the rest of us?

Preparation

Once on board any vessel, immediately find out where the life-jackets are stowed, and try putting one on. You do not want to waste precious time trying to find them, then working out the various straps and buckles in the event of a genuine emergency.

Walk around the ship and get to know the layout, stairways, etc. Make a note of all the exits, and memorize how to reach them, and where they lead to. This could be life-saving knowledge when the lights go out, and cold sea-water starts coming in, blocking off some of the main routes to the upper deck.

Key idea

Having a pre-packed 'grab bag' can be very advantageous if you have to abandon ship at short notice.

Always have a buoyant, waterproof grab bag to hand, which contains survival items for use in either a raft, or on an uninhabited island or coastline. Always customize its contents to your circumstances, but consider packing the following:

- flares
- heliograph or mirror
- emergency distress beacon
- fishing kit
- dry clothing
- compass
- knife
- torch

- high-calorie food
- drinking water
- small telescope or binoculars
- medical kit

I would strongly suggest keeping the smaller items on you, or in your pockets, at all times.

If a grab bag is inappropriate, or if you don't have time to retrieve it, snatch an extra woollen jumper and fill your pockets with sweets and chocolates as quickly as you can. Apart from drowning, your immediate danger will be the cold.

Abandoning ship

Only leave a sinking ship if remaining on board is too dangerous. The second the alarm is heard, put on a life jacket, pick up your grab bag, and get to the open deck as quickly as possible.

Ideally you want to remain as dry as possible, and step from the sinking vessel straight onto the life raft. Do not jump into the sea unless you really have to, and do not jump onto a raft below: you may damage it, yourself, or injure the people already on it. If you must jump, jump clear of any debris or oil/diesel slicks. Lock your legs closed, and hold your nose.

Remember this

If you have an inflatable life-jacket, don't inflate it until you are in the water.

Once off the vessel, you must now do everything you can to get out of the water and into a life raft or onto the shore.

Heat loss

The body's heat loss can be so sudden that it can cause heart failure. If you are a frequent sea traveller you can try to counter this risk by regular exposure to cold water – taking sea swims, cold baths, etc. This will accustom the body to cold water, and so help reduce the effects of the sudden shock and potential heart failure.

The 'heat escape lessening position' (HELP) reduces heat loss by covering the major heat-loss areas. Basically, you must cross your legs and draw them up to your chest, and then wrap your arms around yourself. By being small and ball-like, heat loss is slowed down. You may not always be able to adopt this position, but remember the principles, as heat loss is a major killer in these situations.

Swimming in cold water accelerates cooling. Swim only if the distance is not too great and when you believe you have no better option. All movement increases your heart rate and, as calories are burned, you feel temporarily warmer. However, once that initial heat is lost, you risk cooling down to a dangerous level unless you have the means of getting out of the water and re-warming.

If in a group, bunch together with your arms over each other's shoulders to form a tight rugby scrum-type circle. Put the more vulnerable in the middle for extra warmth. This position is useful in many ways as it keeps everyone a bit warmer, increases your visibility to rescuers, boosts morale, and makes you less attractive to sharks.

Remember this

While in the water, keep all your clothes on (woollen clothes are better in wet conditions at retaining warmth), as well as your shoes.

Protect your neck and head where possible with scarves and hats, as heat loss will be worsened otherwise. Clothing will not drag you down, and will instead act like a wetsuit and keep you a bit warmer. The cold kills.

Staying afloat

You must make every attempt to ensure you have a life-jacket *before* you abandon ship. If none are available, or if you have too little time to find one, you must improvise. Gather up debris, and swim over to anything floating in the water. Treading water will fatigue you, accelerate heat loss, and will be hard to keep up for long. Hypothermia will quickly follow. Trap air in your clothes if you can, and keep all your buttons done up to slow the air's escape. Get out of the water at your first opportunity. You lose heat many times faster in water than in air.

Life rafts

Look after the raft. If it is rubber, do not over inflate it, and be aware of the risk of punctures. Use what you can to stay close to the sunken ship: it probably sent off an SOS call and rescuers could be on their way. Also, your ship would most likely have been in a shipping lane, which means other ships will be passing by. Throw overboard buckets (or a bundle of clothes if you can spare them) on a length of rope and tied to the raft; they will act as anchors and slow your travel.

Once on the raft, wring out wet clothes, and keep the risk of hypothermia uppermost in your mind. Death by hypothermia and dehydration are the most likely causes of death. Wear or share dry clothing with other survivors. Give first aid where you can. Having able-bodied people with you may improve your chances of survival by being able to share out key tasks, keep watch for rescuers and dangers, and raise morale.

It is sometimes advisable to tie yourself to the raft if the sea is rough. Your other concerns are protecting yourself from the sun, the cold and the sea-water – the latter can cause painful boils, which are best prevented by keeping salt off your skin.

Since life rafts are not very manoeuvrable, only try to paddle to the shore early on while you still have the energy, and if it is truly within reach. Take stock of your water and food supplies, and check what other kit and flares are available. Tune into your new environment and make a plan of action.

WATER

Remember this

Before a water supply runs out, try collecting dew and rainwater by stretching out sheets of plastic. Periodically drain it off into containers before sea-spray contaminates it.

Do not drink seawater under any circumstances. In cold conditions, older blue-grey ice can be used for drinking water – suck it like an ice lolly, or allow it to melt in a container.

Good marine suppliers can sell you hand-operated devices which de-salinate sea-water. These handy bits of kit should be in your rafts, and frequent mariners should ensure they always pack one. You can last several weeks without food, but only a few days without water.

Conserve what water you have by drinking nothing for the first 24 hours, then about half a litre for the next three or four days. Finally reduce to a quarter of a litre a day. You will feel rotten, but might just stay alive. Stay clothed and rest. Smoking and alcohol should be avoided. Stop talking, as water – as a vapour – is lost every time you open your mouth.

Food

Remember this
Do not eat unless you have a water supply, as digestion requires water.

Use a fishing kit early on while you still have some strength. Fish often collect under the shade of the raft. At night you can attract fish with a torch. Fish can also be netted if they come close enough. Birds can sometimes be caught by throwing a baited hook and line in the air. Fish are preferable, as they are more palatable raw; remember that everything caught will have to be eaten uncooked.

Case study
The longest anyone has survived afloat in a life raft at sea stands at 133 days. It is the amazing accomplishment of a Chinese steward, on board a merchant vessel in the Atlantic Ocean.

Poon Lim was on board the *SS Ben Lomond,* a British merchant ship, travelling on its own. It had left Cape Town and was heading to the coast of South America. Unfortunately for the ship, it was 1942 and an enemy submarine torpedoed it; it sank, taking many of the crew with it. Eleven people survived. Ten were spotted and picked up, but Poon Lim was left behind.

Poon Lim had managed to grab a life-jacket before having to jump overboard. He floated about for several hours before coming across a life raft; he quickly swam over to it and climbed in. There was no one else in it, and he was alone.

It was a wooden life raft, and fortunately reasonably well stocked with emergency rations, water, flares and a torch. Poon Lim calculated that by careful rationing, he should be able to stay alive for about a month. As the weeks went by, he realized that rescue was increasingly unlikely, and that he needed to start gathering more food and water if he was to survive.

He removed the canvass covering on his life-jacket and used it to catch rain water. He used a biscuit tin, nails and bits of wire from the torch to make fish hooks and cutting edges, banging them into shape with a jug. He unravelled some rope as fishing line. He initially used pieces of precious survival biscuit as bait. After many failed attempts, he caught a fish. He gutted the fish with his rudimentary blade, ate the flesh raw, and used the entrails as bait for the next fishing attempt. In time, he perfected his technique and even managed to catch himself a small shark.

Poon Lim drank the blood from the fish he caught, and varied his diet by catching gulls too. He tried to exercise his legs with the occasional swim, but was constantly on the lookout for sharks. He was spotted twice by passing ships, but never rescued.

Eventually a fishing boat off the Brazilian coast came upon him. By now Poon Lim was unable to walk without support, and had lost nearly ten kilos in body weight. The fishermen carried him aboard, and headed back to land. After a spell in hospital, he made a full recovery.

The full details and background to this incredible sea survival story can be read in *Sole Survivor* by Ruthanne Lum McCunn.

Dangers

The most likely risks to your well-being in these situations are the cold and dehydration. However, there are threats from sea creatures, and although attacks are relatively rare, you should take evasive action when at risk.

Sharks – they are attracted to weak movements, thinking them an easy meal. Do not allow anything body-like to drag in the water (e.g. a blanket hanging over the side of a raft). Sharks are attracted to blood and body wastes from a considerable distance away, and are normally night feeders. Try repelling them with loud noises or sharp jabs with a paddle to the eyes, snout or gills. Use a commercial shark repellent if you have one.

Barracuda – they are attracted to anything shiny or light-coloured in the water. Like sharks, they home in on blood. Cover any watches or jewellery, and try to avoid putting blood into the water around you.

Jelly fish – staying fully clothed will reduce the risk of a nasty sting. However, if you are stung, carefully remove the tentacles with a stick or piece of cloth. Do not rub the wound but wash it with urine, soap or lemon juice.

Signalling

Several rafts tied together will increase your visibility to airborne rescuers. Use brightly-coloured flares where possible, saving any magnesium flares for night-time use. Mirrors and heliographs can be very effective. Mobile phone, laser pointers and distress beacons are clearly helpful if you have them. Preserve battery life, so do not use any devices you have too liberally. Special dyes exist to colour the water to help visibility if an aerial search is likely. If packing your own boat, take some and store with the grab bag or in the life raft.

Signs of land ahead

If floating in the sea, or in a life raft, you may have little control over where the current takes you and it may be a pointless waste of valuable calories to swim or paddle unless you are sure which way to go. However, if you do know where the land lies, it may be worth making the effort to swim or paddle in the right direction. Signs of approaching land include:

▶ Cumulus clouds (white and fluffy), as they form over land.

▶ Birds rarely travel more than about 100 miles from land. Note the direction of travel as many birds fly out over the sea in the morning (looking for food), and back to land in the afternoon.

▶ Insects indicate land is close by. If mosquitoes or flies are starting to find you, it may be a good sign.

▶ Water changes colour. Muddy, silty water might be from an estuary.

▶ Debris and plant matter occur in greater quantities near the coast.

Where possible, notice the signs, and you will therefore notice the changes to those signs. Knowing when to use conserved energy and to start swimming or paddling, rather than just floating, could determine your survival.

Focus points

✳ Know the layout of any ship you board, especially where rafts and life jackets are stowed.

✳ Prepare an emergency waterproof grab bag, full of useful survival items.

✳ Do not jump into a life raft, otherwise you may damage it, yourself, or others – jump in the water next to the raft instead.

✳ Tie yourself to the raft to avoid being thrown out in bad weather.

✳ Start collecting food and water before you need them.

✳ Notice the colour of the sea, the clouds, and bird movements. Look for changes, as they could be indicators of land ahead.

Next step

For completeness, you now need to know about air travel. Many of us now take flights in order to start our outdoor adventure and statistically, the more flights, the more accidents. Modern technology has not been able to stop human error, flocks of birds or lightning strikes, and these all cause aircraft to crash. However, there are ways to survive.

16

Travelling by air

In this chapter you will learn:

▶ *That there are preparations you can make to enhance your chances of survival in the event of a mid-air disaster*

▶ *What to take and wear on an aircraft to improve your survival chances*

▶ *What to do if the plane crashes*

▶ *How being proactive could save your life*

Although air travel is not an outdoor survival skill as such, so many of us take flights in order to start an adventure, mountain climb or expedition, that it is worth noting some survival tips and preparations which might come in useful.

Too many aircraft still crash or fail despite enormous advances in technology and safety. Passengers have been flung into the air while thousands of metres up and survived. Many people have survived plane crashes at sea and over land. Taking personal safety and survival seriously is an effort too few people can be bothered with. The odds of being involved in a mid-air accident are slim, and this comforts enough people into doing nothing.

You are *never* helpless, even when thousands of metres up in the air. You can still give yourself the edge and survive situations others may see as hopeless.

Preparations on the ground

You do need to get to the airport at least two hours before your flight to allow time for security checks. Also, the earlier you get there, the more chance you have of getting the seat of your choice, having a drink and something to eat, and generally being able to relax. Being less rushed also means you can afford to be more vigilant, and not fall foul of baggage thieves wanting to exploit people's anxiety and disorientation. Board the plane hydrated, fed and relaxed.

Have essential documents, money and medication *on you* at all times, either in a zipped pocket, or in a belt pouch. Your hand luggage should contain some food and water (within security regulations), your camera, and perhaps a few useful bits if your main luggage were to get lost. Airport and aircraft regulations will not allow you to carry a knife on you or in your hand luggage, but If you can carry a survival kit, minus a knife, that could prove useful in an emergency. Carry a knife and other kit in your main bag/case in the hold.

Hydrate yourself on non-gassy, non-alcoholic liquids. Eat on the basis that you will be given inadequate food, and much later than you expected. Pack extra food and water into your hand luggage, if the regulations allow.

Wear non-synthetic clothing that covers all of your arms and legs. This is to aid protection in the event of fire. For the same reason, wear proper shoes or boots. Do not get on the aircraft wearing clothes and footwear only suitable for a beach. Within reason, prepare for the unexpected, and wear clothes that will benefit you in the event of a forced landing, perhaps on water.

Key idea

You may be able to reduce the effects of jet lag by adjusting your eating and sleeping patterns to suit your ultimate destination. Melatonin has been proven to help counter jet lag – speak to your GP. Many aircraft personnel take it to speed up their adjustment to the varying time zones.

Take travel sickness pills in time, if required. Look after yourself, as your survival may depend on your mental and physical alertness and well-being.

Remember this

Always keep a Maglite torch, compass and a credit card sized wallet tool (without a blade – air travel regulations prohibit them) with you on the plane.

Study a map of the area over which you are going to be flying. If you go down, you will have a better idea of where you are, where any sea is, and where safety lies. Charge up your mobile phone, but switch it off in-flight.

Clearly label your baggage that goes into the hold, adding a distinctive strap so you can pick it out from all the other bags of a similar appearance.

Remember this

If you have more than one piece of luggage, or are travelling with a friend, distribute your gear among the various bags. Carry half your friend's clothes and kit, and vice versa. That way if one bag/case goes missing, you haven't lost everything.

Put nothing in the hold that you can't afford to lose. Always have hand luggage, and put in it things you could not do without, or replace: medicines, a small first aid kit, a torch, etc., could all prove vital in an accident, or if you are left with nothing but what you have on you.

Remember this

Try to book a direct flight. More than half of air accidents happen during take off or landing – it therefore pays to limit yourself to just one of each. Several stop-overs mean several risks.

Get to the airport early and check in as soon as you can. It is safer (from criminals) in the departure lounge as everyone there has been checked by security.

Relax, eat and hydrate yourself. Catnap if you can.

In the air

Be aware of the risks of deep vein thrombosis (DVT). Blood clots can form in the lower legs, and can ultimately kill you. Counter the risk by wearing 'flight socks', drinking lots of water and walking around or exercising your feet in your seat as often as you can.

Remember this

Suck sweets to help your sinuses, or pinch your nose and blow.

Make sure you read the safety leaflet, and know where the emergency exits and life-jackets are: your life could depend on your knowing this information in a crisis, when seconds can determine who lives and who dies.

Heavy objects falling out of overhead lockers are a frequent cause of injury, particularly during crash landings and heavy turbulence. Where possible, keep your hand luggage on the floor under the seat in front of you.

Stay strapped in your seat during turbulence, or if the captain says so. In cases where people have survived mid-air explosions, they have often been found still strapped in their seats: the seat acted as protection and, although the odds were against them, survived unbelievable falls. Juliane Koepcke (see Chapter 14), survived her aircraft's mid-air crash into the jungle while still strapped to her seat. She was injured, but survived the fall to earth, and did eventually get herself to safety.

Case study

Young 13-year-old Bahia Bakari was on a flight from Paris to the Comoros Islands in the Indian Ocean with her mother. They were on their way to visit relatives and spend a long, sunny summer on an idyllic island.

The flight was not direct and involved several stop-overs, plus a change of aircraft in Yemen. The aircraft that Bahia and her mother were now on had been banned by France years earlier, as there were concerns about its safety record.

The aircraft crashed into the sea as it approached the airport just north of its final destination. It was night-time, and everyone was thrown into the inky, black sea. The cause of the accident was unclear, and later blamed on pilot error. Bahia had not been able to put on a life-jacket as everything happened so quickly.

Injured and alone, young Bahia found herself clinging to a piece of floating debris in a fuel slick, as the aircraft's petrol tanks had burst. Being a small island, Comoros had no rescue facilities, and there were no Sea King helicopters dispatched to the site. Nine hours after the crash, a ferry was able to get out to the crash site to help where it could. No one could get there any sooner.

The crew of the ferry saw nothing but floating dead bodies and pieces of aircraft. However, someone saw Bahia, still clinging to a piece of wreckage, and apparently still alive. She was pulled out of the sea, and taken back to safety. She had some broken bones, and cuts, but otherwise was not too bad. After a spell in various hospitals, she made a full recovery. Unfortunately, she was the sole survivor.

The risks

▶ **Rapid decompression**

If a window blows out at 10,000 metres there will be a loud
bang as the outside air rushes in and the cabin pressure equalizes
to that on the outside. People and objects not strapped down
may well be sucked out of the plane.

Your oxygen mask should fall down automatically – you have
about 15 seconds to put it on, by 30 seconds you'll probably be
unconscious. You will be breathing pure oxygen as air at this
altitude contains too little oxygen to enable you to survive, so
don't remove your mask or move around.

To slow down the effects of rapid decompression, aircraft
windows are normally quite small. Concorde had tiny windows
and flew much higher than normal commercial traffic at around
15–18,000 metres. However, even if breathing pure oxygen, this
is too high to survive if the windows blew out. The barometric
pressure is so low that there is insufficient room in the lungs to
accommodate the required amounts of oxygen. Furthermore,
at over 15,000 metres body fluids will start to vaporize at body
temperature. As you may know, the boiling point of a liquid
drops as you ascend, and by 18,000 metres or so, your blood
will turn to steam and you will simply be boiled to death in
your own body fluids. Not good.

▶ **Crash landings**

As mentioned before, more than half of all aircraft crashes
occur during take off or landing: 70 per cent are survivable,
yet 71 per cent of fatalities occur *after* the plane has stopped
moving. People die in their seats from smoke, fire and injury
because they are waiting for 'someone' to help them or tell them
what to do. Help yourself by being proactive. Several studies
have been carried out on who survives during boat and aircraft
accidents. A common finding is that extroverts, who act without
being told what to do, survive. Too many are paralysed by the
shock and unexpectedness of what has suddenly happened.
Break out of this stunned state, and escape from that which will
soon kill you.

Remember this

Read the safety leaflet, watch the video. Note the emergency exits, and keep your seat belt on.

In the event of a crash landing, bend forward in your seat, with one arm across your knees. Place a pillow or something soft on your lap and hold your head against it with your free arm. Push your legs forward and brace for impact by placing your feet or knees against the chair in front. Statistically, the safer place to sit in order to survive crash landings is towards the rear of the plane. If you get to the airport early, ask for a rear seat.

The airlines with a good history of safety to date include British Airways, Air Canada, Finnair and Qantas. However, things change, so go online and check for the latest list of safe airlines – always assuming you have a choice and several airlines fly to your destination.

▶ Hijacking

Sadly, other human beings represent a risk to us when flying. Smaller airports away from the capital, perhaps only operating internal flights, may have lower security and therefore be more attractive to hijackers and terrorists. Hijackers prefer a manageable amount of people, and so a large two-tier 747 may be avoided in favour of a smaller aircraft.

People sitting in aisle seats are more likely to be pulled out by terrorists and used as sacrificial examples. Fade, and become the invisible 'grey man'. Do not speak or make eye contact with the hijackers, and hide any passport or ID you may have on you. Being a resident of certain countries and having certain professions may antagonize hijackers for obvious, or less obvious, reasons. Do nothing to draw attention to yourself and stay calm but alert. In the majority of cases it is best to trust the negotiators and rescue team and not to intervene. However, there may be some situations where rushing the hijackers with a couple of like-minded passengers may be entirely appropriate, particularly if you believe they are on a suicide mission with nothing to lose. The difficult decision will be yours.

Don't use your mobile phone, as you may be killed if found out. The authorities will have been notified anyway. Some countries have a policy of shooting down aircraft intent on crashing into civilians, so if you call someone, and alert the outside world to the situation, you may risk being shot out of the sky. If you believe or know this to be the case, attempting to overpower the hijackers would probably be appropriate.

Note on parachuting: Perhaps like some of you, I have done a parachute course and jumped into thin air. However, commercial flights do not carry parachutes. Such training is therefore redundant, so do not worry if you lack parachute experience. Jumping out of a burning plane is not always the option you may imagine.

Airport security

As a result of the September 11th attacks, airport security is tighter and consequently getting onto your plane takes a lot longer and involves several body and baggage checks.

Never lose sight of your baggage. Thieves will be waiting for you to fall asleep or become distracted. Drug smugglers will be looking for bags to plant their wares in then retrieve them at the other side. If drugs are found in your baggage, certain countries will impose the death penalty and will not necessary believe you when you say they've been planted. They've heard it all before, and may relish the opportunity of making an example of someone. Make sure your baggage label conceals your home address, as some criminals hang around airports hoping to catch sight of a traveller's address, so they know of an empty home to burgle undisturbed.

At high-risk airports where you believe bombs could be a threat, stay away from anything that could conceal a bomb: bins, telephone booths, etc. Avoid sitting near large expanses of glass, soldiers, and any areas you think a terrorist might target.

Survival in these situations often depends on a capacity to be continually suspicious. Are porters and taxi drivers really what they claim? Did your company/friend really send a car to meet you? Why did that man put a shopping bag in the bin?

Stand at the start of the baggage reclaim carousal, so no one can 'accidentally' take your luggage off before you. Take public transport into town, or a licensed taxi if you feel you can trust the driver. Judgement, and reading people and situations, are understated survival skills.

Focus points

✳ Aircraft crashes do happen, but you can make some preparations to increase your chances of survival.

✳ Take a survival kit, minus a knife, onto the plane.

✳ Wear appropriate clothing and footwear on the plane.

✳ Counter jet lag and travel sickness on long flights as best you can.

✳ Be proactive in the event of a crash, and get out before being told what to do.

✳ Consider your fellow human beings as one of the risks at airports and on the flight.

Next step

Wherever you go, there will be other animals, including insects, which see you either as a danger or as a food source. The rivers and seas have many hazardous residents, the air is alive with life-threatening insects, and the land itself is teeming with threats to your safety. Knowing how to deal with them can mean the difference between life and death.

17

Dealing with animals

In this chapter you will learn:

▶ *How to prevent and treat insect bites*
▶ *Where snakes and scorpions are found*
▶ *How to deal with dangerous mammals, such as big cats and bears*
▶ *How to deal with dangerous dogs*
▶ *How to treat mammal bites to reduce infection and rabies*

If you spend long enough in the outdoors, sooner or later you are going to be pestered or threatened by the wildlife. Fortunately, with some basic preparations and knowledge of their habits, animal encounters need not be threatening.

Note: Dealing with dangerous fish is covered in Chapter 15 on survival at sea.

Insects

Insects are by far the most numerous animals you will encounter, and being able to deal with them can be a real advantage. Apart from delivering nasty stings and bites which can then become infected, many insects also transmit potentially fatal diseases, such as malaria and yellow fever.

▶ Ticks

Found worldwide, especially in forests. They can carry a wide range of diseases including Lyme Disease, which can affect you neurologically as well as physically. Ticks are often picked up as you brush past vegetation, at which point they crawl off looking for flesh to bite into. They swell up as they suck your blood, making them easier to see. Wear gaiters and long trousers, preferably pre-treated with a repellent which should be reapplied daily. Check yourself regularly and carefully remove any ticks with tweezers or special tick cards that many outdoor shops supply.

Remember this

Carry a tick removal card or special tick removal tweezers in your wallet/ pocket at all times. They are inexpensive, and most outdoors shops sell them.

▶ Mosquitoes

Mosquitoes are also found more or less worldwide, but the lethal malaria-carrying type is rarely found outside the tropics. Reduce the chances of being bitten by covering up as much as possible – wear long sleeves and trousers – as well as wearing a repellent with a high DEET content. The female feeds at dusk and this is the worst time to be exposed. Sleep under a net (which you can also treat with a wash-in repellent). Mosquitoes and many other insects do not like smoke or wind, so bear this in mind when camping out. Take anti-malarials, and carry a course of quinine tablets to counter malaria if you succumb to this deadly disease.

▶ Bees and wasps

It appears bees are attracted to the carbon dioxide we exhale as well as light and food (not just sweet things). You will not be able to out-run them, and diving into water won't help as they have been known to wait until the person resurfaces. Turpentine seems to repel them pretty well, but commercially available wasp and bee repellents are available. Treat bites with antihistamine tablets and an anti-sting cream like Anthisan. Bee stings are acidic and the effects can be countered with an alkali, like toothpaste. Wasp stings are alkaline, and can be countered with a mild acid, such as vinegar.

Key idea

Ice will relieve the pain and swelling of most bites and stings.

Snakes and scorpions

Although snake and scorpion venom can be fatal, the quantity they inject is usually too small to be lethal to an average adult, unless they are ill or elderly. The amount of venom injected is designed to kill or harm smaller animals that are likely threats and potential food sources. Useful tips when dealing with snakes and scorpions include:

▶ Research the area and know what to expect *before* you get there.

▶ Carry a venom extractor and/or anti-venom for the snakes known to be in the area.

▶ Be cautious of sunny spots in a forest: snakes may be sunning themselves.

- Be aware of snakes hanging down from branches and curled around trees.

- Snakes and scorpions are often found under rocks and logs.

- Most snake bites are below the knee, so wear adequate boots, gaiters and long trousers.

- Stamp your feet or bang the ground with a heavy walking stick as you enter 'snake territory' as this may scare them off; many bites occur because snakes are startled or accidentally trodden on.

- Seal any uncooked meats you may have with you, as snakes and other animals are attracted to them.

- Sleep off the ground. Insects, scorpions and snakes will bother you less, particularly as some are heat seeking. Shake out all clothes and boots every morning.

The treatment of snake bites depends on the type of snake. If you are able to identify the snake, or even catch it, this will help any medics to administer the correct antidote. If you are alone, without an antidote, here are the basic principles:

- Stay calm and sit down, ensuring the bite is lower than the heart. The faster your heartbeat, the quicker the venom circulates around your body and does its damage

- Tie a tight bandage above the bite site to restrict the flow of venom further into the body. If a very tight tourniquet is left in place for a long time it will cause damage to the limb and you will risk amputation. This course of action may be necessary however in the case of bites from cobras, mambas and poisonous Australian snakes.

- Use a venom extractor if you have one. If you are going to an area where poisonous snakes are found, buy one from an outdoor supplier before you go, they are not difficult to get, or bulky to carry. Sucking the venom out is not recommended: venom may still enter the bloodstream via broken skin in your gums, tongue or cheeks, or perhaps by your not spitting it all out of your mouth. The stuff of Tarzan films, but not a real survival situation.

- Clean the wound and apply ice to ease the pain and swelling.

Mammals

Most mammals naturally fear humans and will keep away. However, they may attack if:

- surprised
- hungry
- ill or injured
- with their young
- you have walked into their territory

You will be less detectable if you remain as scentless as possible by:

- Not washing for three to four days beforehand.
- Not using any toiletries.
- Ensuring clothes are not freshly washed and reeking of detergent.
- Walking on hard, stony ground where possible.
- Staying upwind once you know where the dangerous animals are.
- If you chance upon a dangerous animal very close by, staying near to the ground and reducing the risk of letting the wind carry your scent towards the animal.
- If resting for a while, cover yourself with a large poncho or similar, to stop your scent wafting into the airstreams and alerting animals you wish to avoid.
- Travelling in very windy, wet or cold conditions, as scent is harder to detect.

Although many animals have poor eye sight and rely heavily on scent and sound, you should still try to remain unseen. It is easier to see fast-moving animals than it is to see very slow moving ones.

If remaining invisible is simply not possible or feasible, focus instead on being noisy and not surprising the animal.

Key idea

Some animals attack if startled, but given warning of your presence may well move off and keep out of your way.

BEARS

Find out when the bears in the country/region you are visiting hibernate and give birth to their cubs. Bears are most dangerous just before they go into hibernation and again when their cubs are born. Here is how to avoid them:

▶ As with all potentially dangerous mammals you think you might encounter in the area you are going in to, know their prints, habitat, eating signs, smell, habits, and what their droppings look like.

▶ Travel in a group, as bears are more likely to attack lone individuals.

▶ Be prepared to drop your pack or a bag containing food as a distraction to enable you to escape.

▶ Be noisy to give them a chance to move away.

▶ Avoid using any perfumed toiletries, sun-creams, etc., as bears may mistake the scent for food.

▶ Seal all food in plastic bags and boxes and store well away from your campsite, perhaps suspended from a tree. You are advised to cook and eat at least half a mile away from your eventual campsite. Bears have a phenomenal sense of smell and will seek you out from many miles away. Wash thoroughly after eating and try not to get any food on your clothes. Bury all rubbish.

▶ Cover any injuries as bears can smell blood very easily.

▶ Use bear repellents if available and ensure you spray around your tent every night. You should also consider running a fence (length of cord on sticks) around your campsite, on which alarms or noisy tin cans are suspended. Anything knocking into the fence will set off the alarm, and make a noise. This may not frighten the animal off, but may at least buy you enough time to take evasive action and escape.

► If a bear does confront you, some experts suggest raising your hand (or hands) palms to the bear in a 'halt' style position. Shaking out a black plastic bin-liner also has reports of effectiveness. Most agree to standing your ground and *not* running off – you could never out-run a bear anyway and they can climb trees easily. Those who have encountered grizzlies suggest playing dead. Regretfully, there is no guaranteed method of preventing an attack.

BIG CATS

Avoidance is as for bears: they normally move off if they hear and see you coming. Do not show fear, start to run or back off. If you come upon a large cat, try making yourself look big by opening your jacket and holding the sides open so that you appear larger. In the absence of a firearm, throwing rocks, using a flare, catapult or spear may scare them off. Appearing big, noisy and a potential threat are often the best way of dealing with them.

DOGS

Dogs are everywhere and many are bred to be aggressive, and then trained to attack certain people in a particular way. Here is how to avoid them and hopefully prevent being bitten:

► Carry an electric dog repeller. These small hand-held devices send out ultrasonic sounds which dogs find painful and repel most dogs – more so if accompanied by a loud, sharp command like 'sit!' They can be bought directly from the manufacturer (www.dazer.com), via the internet, or from a pet shop.

► Dogs are more aggressive in the heat.

► Do not threaten a dog if it is in your way: go around it and speak softly.

► Packs of dogs are more aggressive than one dog on its own.

► Avoid dogs while they are eating or fighting among themselves. It may not take much for them to turn on you.

► If confronted by a hostile dog, stand your ground and avoid eye contact. Do not show signs of weakness, fear or start to run away.

Case study

For wildlife conservationist, Greg Rasmussen, the animals turned the tables round, and made him the focus of their attention instead of the other way round. He very nearly became the next meal for several different species he was meant to be studying.

He had been flying alone over one of Zimbabwe's national parks in a fragile microlight aircraft, monitoring rhino movements. Some 70 miles from the nearest road, and a thousand feet up, the small aircraft stalled, and crash-landed.

Rasmussen suffered badly from the crash. He had fuel pouring over him waiting to ignite, as well as two broken legs, broken ribs and a cracked pelvis. He could not walk at all, and crawling was too painful. The crash had happened so suddenly, that he had been unable to fire off a Mayday call. No one knew where he was, or that he needed urgent help.

Rasmussen crawled around the broken aircraft to the radio, and tried to call for help, but the radio was not working. His situation started to get worse. A herd of elephants came close by, and appeared not to detect the injured man. Rasmussen remained perfectly quiet, thinking a sudden noise or movement might panic the elephants and cause them to stampede or come even closer.

Fortunately, the elephants passed, but then came a curious lion. The tactic this time, since he had already been seen by the lion, was to startle it and try to frighten it off once it got close. With all his might, Rasmussen banged against the wreckage and made as much noise as he could. The lion, now only yards away, recoiled at the sudden explosion of sound, and went away.

Rasmussen was not in good shape, and watched vultures start to gather around him. Soon a hyena found him too. Fortunately, the lion trick worked again, and Rasmussen's sudden explosion of banging and loud noise saw it off. As night fell, and the many nocturnal animals came out, Rasmussen remained as vigilant as ever.

He survived the night, and in the morning thought he would retry the broken radio. It worked! He radioed for help, and gave his approximate location. As he had had to stay with the aircraft, he was relatively easy to see from the air. The rescuers found him, and he was taken to hospital. After much treatment, he made a full recovery and continued with his conservation work in Africa.

Remember this

Get a rabies and tetanus jab if travelling to areas where rabies is known to occur. Note – dogs are not the only animal that can give you rabies, so even if you think you're unlikely to come into contact with dogs, the jabs are still worth having. Combined with tetanus, these inoculations offer some very beneficial protection against unwanted bites.

If a dog appears intent on biting you, try offering it a padded/protected arm to bite. This allows you to control the dog to an extent, and gives you the opportunity to kick or punch its throat, cosh or stab it. You should note that some police and military dogs are trained not to hold on once they have bitten you, but instead to make several quick bites. If you do decide to attack a dog, rather than try to defend yourself against it, do so with maximum force and plenty of noise.

The treatment for mammal bites and cuts is to wash the wound thoroughly in soapy water, putting the wound under running water for at least a few minutes to try and flush out as much unwanted material as possible. Remove any broken claws or teeth from the wound and then irrigate it with either alcohol of at least 40 per cent proof, a powerful antiseptic or iodine. Normal antiseptics are less effective. Bandage the wound and get a rabies and/or tetanus jab as soon as possible. Antibiotics should also be taken as the dirty teeth and claws of mammals cause bacterial infections easily.

Focus points

* Treat insects seriously and do what you can to prevent being bitten.
* Carry a venom extractor into areas habited by snakes and/or scorpions.
* Avoid dangerous mammals by masking your scent and staying upwind of them.
* Ice, or something cold, soothes irritating bites and stops you scratching.
* Wash all bites with lots of soapy water for several minutes to combat infection.
* Learn as much about the wildlife and insects you may encounter before you get there. Habitat, eating habits, tracks and sign, when they have their young, when they are most active, etc. This knowledge may reduce your risk of attack.

Next step

By this stage you will have acquired a good foundation knowledge of survival techniques. You will also have picked up some more specialist skills that further extend your freedom. These will enable you to go to increasingly remote places for longer periods. It is now time to look at survival in particular environments, starting with the seashore.

18

Seashore survival

In this chapter you will learn:

▶ *About ways of surviving along a seashore*
▶ *Signalling methods to aid rescuers*
▶ *How to find food and water along a seashore*
▶ *The importance of preparation*

Disaster has struck. Your plane has gone down, your ship has sunk. You have made it to the shore, but only have the clothes that you stand up in. To enable rescuers to see you, and for you to see them, you decide to remain on the seashore. Here are some tips on surviving long enough to be rescued.

Remember this

In all survival situations, you need to act quickly. The effects of cold, fatigue, shock and injury can all inhibit your thinking and prevent you from acting properly. Before long, food and water deprivation also take their toll and you will soon be fit for nothing. Speed is essential; put a plan of action in place before you are unable to think and act constructively.

Salvage what you can from your disaster and get out of the water. For the next 24 hours your concerns are warmth, signalling, shelter, water and food.

Warmth

Remember this

Wring out your clothes as soon as you can. Being in the water will have lowered your body temperature and you need to counter the possible effects of hypothermia as soon as possible. If the air temperature is warm enough, strip off and dry your clothes.

If damp clothes have to be worn, stuff grass or any dry vegetation between the layers of your clothes. Wet clothing is heat sapping if directly next to the skin. The space created will enable wet clothes to dry quicker and will create a warm layer of air around you.

Keep moving, as sitting still in cold, wet clothing will both lower your morale and your already low body temperature. Get out of the wind and take stock of the situation. Ideally you want to get a fire going as soon as you can.

Since much body heat is lost through the head and neck, these are areas you should concentrate on wrapping up and protecting.

Signalling

Chances are that your plane/ship sent off a Mayday call before it went down. Rescuers will be looking for survivors: help them to find you. For the first few days, stay near to the coastline and find a highpoint.

Prepare a large fire by having all of the necessary tinder, kindling and larger wood to hand (see Chapter 4). You also want something that produces smoke. Any rubber or plastic will produce black smoke, whereas wet wood or leaves will produce white smoke. Have regard to what is behind and around you, and decide what might be easier to see if you were a ship a mile or so off-shore. If you have plenty of materials, and for speed and ease, consider keeping a fire going continuously.

Remember this
Practise fire lighting before you need it.

In addition to your fire, you should also try attracting potential rescuers' attention by flashing them with something shiny, or by waving a large piece of cloth once the ship gets a little closer.

Try making a large X or SOS from debris/vegetation, or by digging trenches in the shape of the letters to cast shadows on light coloured sand.

Key idea
All forms of signalling are made more effective if you can contrast the background.

Obviously, torches or flares would be handy but life is rarely kind enough to bestow useful kit on you when you actually need it! Improvisation and resourcefulness are the keys to survival.

With the possible exception of gun shots, the sound of the wind and waves make the coast too noisy to rely upon a loud noise being heard. Instead, I would suggest that attempts to attract rescuers are based on several visual aids being used simultaneously. Never rely on just one signal being seen.

Shelter

The kind of shelter needed depends on your estimate of how long you are going to have to survive until rescued. Always, however, use natural features to reduce the work. Conserve calories and materials and make lean-tos, use caves, etc., rather than building a four-walled hut from scratch.

Obviously stay well beyond the high-tide mark. Look for signs of tide marks and debris to see how far the sea comes in. Avoid lying directly on sand dunes, particularly if plants or grass are growing through. Irritating biting insects are likely to be present. Where possible, try to get off the ground and consider a make-shift platform or hammock as a bed. If nothing else, you will be warmer if you can put something between you and the heat-sapping ground; even lying on a bed of twigs or pile of palm leaves will help. See also Chapter 5.

Water

Remember this

Sea-water must not be drunk. In sufficient quantities it will cause kidney failure and death. By all means pour saltwater over yourself to keep cool (and so lessen dehydration) but never drink it.

There are several water sources along a seashore to consider. Try these:

Plants: Coconuts are the prime source of a safe liquid from plants in tropical climates. The green ones contain more milk than the older ones, but be aware of the laxative effect. The chunky white flesh makes a good food source, but the tough husk around the actual shell can be difficult to remove. In the absence of a heavy knife, you can normally open them by bringing them down hard on a strong sharpened stick securely staked in the ground, or the edge of a sharp rock.

In the absence of coconuts, try gathering dew on grasses and plants. This can be done by mopping up the dew with an absorbent cloth, simply by dragging the cloth through the plants, and then wringing it out into a container.

Well: Dig a well approximately a hundred metres above the high-tide mark. The brackish water can be made more palatable by passing it through a filter, such as a sock filled with sand.

Distillation: Boil up some sea-water and then cover the container with an absorbent cloth so that the (salt free) steam is caught. Wring out the cloth into a separate container.

Key idea

Water is more important than food and should be a priority. As with signalling, employ several methods simultaneously to maximize your chances of success.

Food

Food sources along a shoreline include fish, birds, shellfish and plants.

▶ Fish

There are many fish that frequent the shallow waters near the shore, as well as any estuaries nearby. These include salmon, herring, tarpon and turbot. Try catching them by any of the following methods:

▶ Hook and line: use a cord (e.g. the inner threads of paracord) and an improvised hook. Use shellfish, insects, worms or dead fish as bait. As many fish swallow their food whole, you can even try tying a small piece of thorny stick to your cord if you have nothing to use as a hook. This may enable you to land the fish before it is able to dislodge the barbed stick and spit it out.

▶ Netting: make a net by opening part of the bottom seam of a T-shirt and threading it on to the forks of a Y-shaped branch. Tie the ends of the branch together, and close the shirt opening with a bootlace.

▶ Trapping and spearing: using rocks and sticks, create a bottle neck in a stream or shallow area forcing the fish into a narrow enough passage so that you can either spear or net them.

Try it now

Familiarize yourself with the shellfish along a seashore near you. Gather and eat what you find. Take away the uncertainty, and you will be better prepared if you have to do it in a real survival situation.

▶ Birds

Sea birds are often very large and make a worthwhile meal. You can catch them using baited hooks, spearing or stoning. One easy method that sometimes works is to wrap some bait around a stone and toss it into the air towards a bird in flight. The unexpected weight can often make the bird drop to the ground, whereupon you can club or catch it. Snares, particularly those that are spring-loaded, trigger a crushing weight or spear, or encase the bird are also effective.

▶ Shellfish

Most seashores have several types of shellfish, including mussels, limpets and razorshells. Only collect live ones and always boil them as soon after you have collected them as you can. Boil for at least five minutes. Discard any mussels that do not open after boiling and avoid any shellfish near any source of pollution. Crabs are never too difficult to catch and are an excellent food source. Boil for around 15–20 minutes before eating.

▶ Plants

All seashores will have seaweeds which make useful additions to any soups or stews. Kelp and bladderwrack types are very common and, once thoroughly washed in fresh-water, need only be boiled before eating. Alternatively, lay them out to dry then grind to a powder to thicken up your stews.

Eat well and you will have the energy and morale to stay alive and give signalling and shelter-making the proper care and attention it needs. See also Chapter 6.

Case study

The survival story of Scottish sailor Alexander Selkirk was the basis for Daniel Defoe's classic, *Robinson Crusoe*. In the early 1700s Selkirk had serious concerns about the seaworthiness of the ship he was working on, and asked the captain whether he could be left behind on one of the islands. He felt sure the leaky ship would sink if it continued any further. His wish was granted, and Selkirk was put ashore on an uninhabited Pacific Ocean island with all his personal effects.

Selkirk was proved right, and his ship did indeed go down off the South American coast, close to what is now called Colombia.

Initially, Selkirk remained along the seashore. He collected and ate shellfish, but also kept watch for rescue, hoping to be picked up by another passing ship. The isolation soon began to trouble him, and he suffered from loneliness and depression. When large groups of noisy and irritating sea lions gathered on the seashore for their mating season, Selkirk decided to move away and explore the island's interior.

The interior offered him a greater variety of food. Wild goats provided him with nutritious meat and milk. He also found vegetables such as turnips, cabbage and black pepper berries. The quality and quantity of his food improved, as did his mental and physical health as a consequence. At first he was disturbed by rats at night, but soon befriended some wild cats (perhaps left by previous passing sailors), and eliminated the problem. He became highly adaptable, and had a healthy, sustainable attitude towards his situation.

He proved extremely resourceful in using items brought from the ship when he was put ashore, as well as materials that he found on the island itself. He combed the beach for useful debris, and managed to make himself a knife out of barrel hoops he found on the seashore. He built himself two huts out of trees. Until his supply of gunpowder ran out, he hunted game with his rifle, and then gutted and prepared them with his newly-made knife.

Selkirk's father had been a tanner, and knew how to turn animal hide into a soft and useable material. When his clothes needed replacing, Selkirk was able to make himself replacements from goatskin, using a nail for sewing. He remained barefoot, allowing his feet to toughen. He found comfort in reading from a Bible he had taken with him. Perhaps not consciously, Selkirk addressed his physical and mental needs, and thereby made his solitary long-term survival on the island sustainable.

Years passed. Unfortunately for Selkirk, the first two ships to stop on his remote island were Spanish, enemies of Britain at the time. Had they found him, they may well have either killed him or captured him. Selkirk rightly feared for his life and hid; the ships and their crews ultimately left the island without him.

After more than four years from the time he was put ashore, a British ship eventually pulled into the island. Although initially startled by Selkirk, they soon welcomed him, and assured him of a safe passage back home. The now quick and agile castaway managed to catch several goats a day for the weary crew, and helped restore their flagging health, as many of them were suffering from the effects of scurvy. Once the crew were back in shape and fully rested, the ship set sail for Britain, and to safety.

It was said by those that met him after his rescue how impressed they were by his tranquillity of mind, as well as by his physical health and the vigour that he had acquired while alone on the island. Some might have argued he was now a better man for his ordeal.

There have been several books about Alexander Selkirk; try *The Life and Adventures of Alexander Selkirk* by John Howell for the background and a fuller account of his story.

Preparation

Prevention is better than cure. You can try to prevent unwanted circumstances befalling you by planning ahead. Prepare by asking yourself 'what if?' and see how ready you are for an accident and a possible change in circumstances. Accept that your fate is down to you, and that no one in authority is going to step in and save you.

Minimize the possibility of hardship, and get into the habit of always carrying a survival kit *on you* – not buried somewhere in your kit, or stowed in a safe place for later.

Key idea

Get into the habit of carrying a Swiss army knife or multi-tool with you at all times. Any journey could result in a crash or breakdown.

Tailor the contents of a pouch survival kit to your circumstances and to the environment you are going to be in. While travelling, have a small but well stocked 'grab bag' ready to snatched when disaster strikes. This should complement your survival kit, and contain food and water, as well as flares, perhaps an emergency rescue beacon, and also a medical kit. It could make the difference between survival and slow death. Pack one and stow it where it can be grabbed at a moment's notice.

Seashores are not barren and devoid of life-supporting opportunities. They offer a wealth of food and survival assistance. By all means keep your shelter and signalling close to the coast, but don't be afraid to forage inland. Fear of the unknown can restrict you so much as to kill you. Look at the survival of Alexander Selkirk (see the case study above) – by going inland and leaving his comfort zone, he radically improved his situation and made long-term survival realistic and almost comfortable.

Remember this

Always look on the positive side and remember, as I was once told, 'you are never defeated until you give up'.

Focus points

* Seashores offer a variety of edible plants and food sources.
* Your immediate priorities if marooned are keeping warm and finding a source of drinkable water.
* Do not be afraid of going inland and exploring the area.
* Build a large smoky fire on a high point, ready to ignite if a ship sails close by.
* Anticipate the possible, and prepare for the worst – having a survival kit and grab bag could save your life if you have to abandon ship.

Next step

Another environment you may need to survive in a jungle or dense forest. Aircraft fly over, and sometimes crash into, large jungles and rainforests. Expeditions and planned hikes through jungles go wrong, and people get injured and/or lost. The jungle is neutral and can be your best friend in these situations, not your enemy.

19

Jungle survival

In this chapter you will learn:

- ▶ *What medical issues to prepare for in a jungle*
- ▶ *About what kit you should take with you*
- ▶ *How best to travel*
- ▶ *About shelter-making in a jungle*
- ▶ *How to deal with insects and the heat*
- ▶ *How to enhance your chances of survival and rescue*

Many of us now travel to the world's jungles as part of an adventure holiday or planned expedition. Some end up in the jungle unexpectedly, as the result of an accident such as a plane crash. I have been to the jungles of three continents, spending five months in the Amazon alone. While the jungle may not actively be out to get you, to the ill-prepared it can be a life-threatening environment. There are a number of dangerous animals, be they insects or snakes, alligators or jaguars.

Medical issues

At least a month or two before you intend going to a jungle, take advice from a medical specialist with expertise in tropical medicine and the up-to-date preventative measures. See Appendix 4 (Taking things further) at the end of this book. Get every jab you can, including rabies – blood sucking vampire bats really do exist in South America, as do vicious dogs guarding remote villages in Nepal.

Many environments, including jungles, do not offer ready access to professional health care or speedy access for rescuers if you need urgent medical attention. In most cases, you are on your own. Your knowledge, skills and equipment may be all that lie between you and death.

You should be prepared to deal with the following:

▶ dehydration

▶ heatstroke

▶ infected cuts

▶ malaria and fevers generally

▶ insect bites, including spiders and scorpions

▶ snake bites – there are a lot of snakes in jungle areas

▶ other animal bites

▶ stomach upset/diarrhoea

▶ pain

Your medical kit should be customized with the above risks in mind. This may make for a large medical kit, but the nature of jungles may mean you need it more than you think. Do not scrimp on antiseptics.

Remember this

Deal with minor cuts, blisters, etc. *immediately* to prevent infection. The humid conditions in the jungle are ripe for bacteria and you need to minimize the risk.

Useful kit

You *must* take a mosquito net to sleep under; they are small, relatively cheap, and really do help prevent malaria-laden mosquitoes from biting you. Other useful kit for jungle situations includes:

▶ Hammock: preferably the type with a sewn-in mosquito net and flysheet covering. Sleeping off the ground is almost essential, because of the proliferation of insect and animal life.

▶ Jungle boots: these are cooler than most boots, dry out quicker, and have specially designed soles that make travel over boggy ground easier.

▶ Water filter and water containers: although finding water should not be a problem, cleaning it and carrying it may be.

▶ Medical kit: see section on medical issues above for what it should contain.

▶ Mobile/cell/satellite phone or other means of communicating with the outside world: check before you leave whether there will be coverage in the area you are visiting.

▶ Compass/GPS and maps: keep these protected in a waterproof map case, and remember to carry spares.

▶ Emergency location beacon: this could simply be a very bright flashing light to catch the eye of a search plane.

▶ Anti-fungal foot powder or cream: the humidity and persistent heat make fungal infections unpleasantly common.

- Cotton hat and head net: these will help keep biting insects at bay.

- Insect repellent: this should preferably contain DEET, simply because it works for many hours before you need to reapply more.

Remember this

Pre-wash shirts and trousers in insect repellent before you arrive in the jungle. Some outdoor companies sell specially treated clothing that has an insect repellent embedded in the material that is very hard to wash out.

- Machete or large knife: don't forget also a means of sharpening it – fire, raft and shelter-making can be very difficult without one.

- Light, cotton clothing: plus spares, especially socks and underwear as even if you are able to wash clothes, getting anything to dry properly in a humid jungle is not always easy.

Remember this

Know your area - research it, familiarize yourself with the common animals, plants, terrain and medical problems that might befall you. Find out how far you would be from a hospital or airport. Check the normal time of year for monsoons and significant weather changes. Do not go to a jungle area unprepared.

Travel

Only travel if you believe that remaining where you are is either dangerous, too concealed to be found by rescuers, or detrimental to your survival in some way. Be conscious of conserving calories and reducing risks.

Travel in daylight and trust your compass. Avoid particularly dense vegetation (which may contain skin-shredding thorns) and accept that going round is far better than trying to hack your way through. Use a stick or a machete to move vegetation and not your hands. Snakes and biting insects are very well camouflaged and will not hesitate to bite anything that threatens them.

Travelling along higher ground and ridges is often easier as there will be fewer streams and swamps to cross and the forest thins a little too, making for easier progress. Be realistic with how much ground you can cover; jungle travel is extremely hard-going. The terrain, the heat and the humidity as well as the plant and animal life means a few miles a day is probably your limit.

Speedier travel may be possible by making a raft and floating downstream. Waterfalls, rapids and dangerous fish, etc. may be worth the risk if you are desperate to find help and get back to safety as quickly as possible.

Key idea

Most towns and villages in jungle areas are either on riverbanks or close to them.

Travel downstream where the river widens and grows in size. Your chances of finding a settlement are more likely as the river increases in size and larger boats can travel.

River crossings

See Chapter 13 on river crossings and raft building. As river crossings are going to be likely in a jungle, waterproof essential kit and anything electrical. Where possible, cross in slow-moving water, away from any rapids or falls. Scout downstream of your intended crossing point to ensure you are not going to float into something hazardous. Aim for a place on the opposite bank that can be climbed up easily. Use a stick to steady yourself and slip one arm out of your rucksack so it can be removed quickly – if you fall, your pack will fill with water and quickly pull you under. Keep survival equipment, including your knife, strapped *to you* at all times as you could easily lose your pack in a river crossing. Plan for the worst, and give yourself a fighting chance if you lose your rucksack.

Don't urinate in rivers within the Amazon Basin as the tiny candiru, a barbed parasitic fish, (sometimes called the toothpick or vampire fish) may be present. These blood-sucking fish are allegedly able to swim up a stream of urine and into you. Not only is the pain unbearable but removal requires surgery. Not common, and may be more exaggeration than fact, but why run the risk?

Piranha fish, alligators, crocodiles, river snakes and hippos could all kill you before you reach the other side so don't hang around. Rivers are convenient highways for many animals, and the river and the riverbank are the home for many more. Don't tempt fate, and get out of the water as soon as you can.

Case study

Yossi Ghinsberg was in a small group of four, travelling in South America. The group had formed in the Bolivian part of the Amazon, and had plans to hike into uncharted jungle, experience real adventure, and find lost tribes and forgotten villages. However, after several weeks of hard going, they still had not reached their destination. They did have a guide, but he was not a local, and after a while they had to fend for themselves. The group fragmented, and Ghinsberg was left with Kevin Gale, an American, to find their own way back. The guide and the fourth member of the group left them and went their own way. They were never seen again.

Ghinsberg and Gale managed to obtain a raft from some villagers; travelling by river is often quicker and safer than slow travel over land. However, they failed to scout ahead, and soon found themselves caught up in very fast-moving water heading for dangerous rocks – and a waterfall. Gale managed to jump out and got to the safety of the riverbank. Ghinsberg went over the falls.

Ghinsberg survived, and even managed to salvage a few bits of kit before heading off into the jungle. Both friends looked for each other, but the distance and the terrain between them made contact impossible; each probably thought the other was dead, and they had to continue alone to find a way to safety.

Ghinsberg wandered for nearly three weeks looking for a village or someone to help him. He suffered terrible injuries to his feet, fell into quicksand, encountered a jaguar, leeches, snakes, and all manner of biting insects. He managed to frighten off the jaguar by spraying some flammable insect repellent through the flame of a lighter, thereby creating a small cloud of flames. He ate fruits where he could, but reached a very low mental state, and seriously doubted his ability to go on. However, he defeated his negative thoughts and stayed alive long enough to be found. Miraculously, his friend Gale had survived too and, with a local boatsman, went searching for Ghinsberg.

After a long spell in hospital, Ghinsberg fully recovered and later returned to live for a while in the same area in which he had become lost. The full story is told in Yossi Ghinsberg's book *Lost in the Jungle*.

Shelter

Note the time that the sun sets and camp well before darkness. Do not camp too near to rivers and swamps – the insects will be prolific enough without worsening the situation. Don't camp underneath any heavy branches, as death and injury from falling dead wood is surprisingly common. Also take into account the likely route of rainwater – flash floods are frequent in jungle areas.

Once you've found a site, carefully clear the undergrowth by sweeping it with a branch, and erect your hammock, if you have one. Do what you can to get off the ground. Kit should be suspended on cord from trees. Being off the ground is drier (particularly during the rains), cooler and gets you and your kit away from insects and other unwanted animal life that may be either dangerous or just irritating.

Dealing with insects

Wear clothing that covers you completely including repellent-treated light-weight gaiters. Mosquitoes and blood sucking leeches rely on exposed flesh for their meals. Always sleep under your netting.

Hats and fine mesh netting over your head are more or less essential. Apply repellent to your clothes and hat. Pre-treat your mosquito net (and hammock), if you can. Some insects lay eggs in wounds or as they bite, so you really do want to repel as many as you can. Once the eggs hatch, they will erupt from a swelling. The discomfort and risk of infection should be avoided if you can.

Shake boots, sleeping bags, rucksacks, hammocks and clothing every time you put them on or pack them away. Insects, snakes, scorpions, and perhaps even rodents, may have found their way in.

Try not to lie or sit on the ground or on logs, even if they appear insect-free. Smoky fires will deter some insects and unwanted guests, and I would suggest you keep one going when you stop to pitch camp.

Take your anti-malarial tablets without fail, and use painkillers and antihistamines to deal with bites. Bite sites should be cleaned and plastered to prevent infection. Look out for bites that swell up after a few days; the insect (e.g. botfly or tumbu fly) may have laid its eggs under your skin only for the maggots to hatch out later.

Dealing with the heat

The humidity and oppressive heat can be unceasing and drain you of energy quickly. Listen to your body and take extra precautions to ensure heatstroke and dehydration are avoided. Wrap a cool wet scarf around your neck, soak your hat in water – do what you can to stay cool. You risk making dangerous mistakes if you let irritability get on top of you.

Symptoms of dehydration and heatstroke include headaches, dizziness, ringing in the ears, nausea, developing into confusion and ultimately a coma. Treat by cooling yourself down (pour water over yourself) and drinking. Take painkillers for any headaches. It is common for the symptoms of heatstroke and dehydration to be so distracting as to cause errors of judgement leading either to injuries or damaged equipment.

Drink frequently. Thirst is a notoriously bad indicator of your fluid needs, particularly in humid conditions. If you can, set a digital watch to beep every hour to ensure you drink regularly. As a rough guide, you need at least two to three litres of fluid in normal temperate climates, per day. In a jungle, trekking throughout the day, don't be surprised if you have to at least triple this.

Wash your feet daily and treat with an anti-fungal powder or cream. Wear fresh socks if you can, every day. Similarly, change your underwear daily. Wash the groin region, and treat with talc or an anti-fungal powder to see off any problems. Fungal complaints as well as prickly heat are both unpleasant and incredibly itchy. These simple steps will go a long way to preventing them.

Cotton clothing is usually better than synthetic material, but unless given an opportunity to dry out, may rot in the jungle from the high humidity. Clothing should be as baggy as practical; the circulating air will help to keep you cool.

Food and drink

The jungle has an abundance of edible plants and animals. Fish can be caught relatively easily using a simple baited hook and line. I have dined on piranha fish a few times, baiting them with pieces of slug. Fruits commonly found include bananas, papayas, wild figs, persimmons, mangoes and various nuts like almonds, brazils and cashews.

Water is usually everywhere and simply needs to be filtered (to remove the sediment), then purified either by boiling or by passing through a water filter. Drinkable water can also be obtained from vines; cut a notch in a vine as high up as you can reach, then cut the end off close to the ground. Drinkable water will start to drip out. Do not suck the vine, it may cause irritation. Avoid anything producing a milky sap.

Water can be also be found trapped inside bamboo stems; shake them and then drill a small hole to let it flow out. Rainwater also collects in the crevices of large-leafed plants and flowers, like the Pitcher plant. After every rainfall, collect as much as you can hold.

Remaining properly hydrated is important, and it may be worth drinking slightly unclean water to do so. Water collected from the middle of a fast-moving stream/river will be cleaner than that gathered near the riverbank.

Rescue

Generally speaking, stay with your vehicle, plane or boat. Your route may have been logged and rescuers will start by retracing it once you fail to arrive. It is far easier to see a vehicle or crashed plane from the air, than to spot a small, lone figure walking through dense jungle.

Signalling is difficult as the dense forest disperses smoke before it reaches the outside world. Try making a smoky fire on a floating platform and push it out into the middle of a river, tethered by a cord so you don't lose it. Alternatively, light a smoky fire in a clearing if you can find one.

A flashing strobe light might be seen if you have one, but the spotter plane would have to be virtually overhead. Again, have it flashing in the middle of a wide, slow-moving river, or in a clearing where it will have more chance of being seen. Depending on where you are, mobile phones and radios may work, but do depend on batteries so will have limited life.

Focus points

* Jungles present a multitude of health risks that you need to prepare for.
* Insects must be taken seriously and repellent and specific medication must form part of your medical kit.
* Food and water sources are plentiful.
* Sleep off the ground wherever possible.
* Signalling can be difficult as smoke may not penetrate the forest canopy. Instead, float a smoky fire on a platform and push it out into the middle of a wide river, or find a clearing.
* Travelling by river is often easier than hacking your way through the dense bushes and trees.

Next step

You do not have to go to the Himalayas or high Andes to have your life and well-being threatened by a mountain. The comparatively smaller peaks in the Alps, Dolomites, and even the Scottish Highlands, claim many lives every year. Mountains present a multitude of risks which you need to be aware of and prepare for.

Mountain survival

In this chapter you will learn:

▶ *What key preparations to make before you go*

▶ *About what to include in your life-saving kit*

▶ *Essential skills for safe mountain travel*

▶ *About the common dangers you may have to face*

Whether you are camping and hiking through the Swiss Alps, the Scottish Highlands, or perhaps on a more serious expedition to the Himalayas or Andes, mountain regions can pose a serious threat to the ill-prepared. The risks are constantly miscalculated, and the extremes of the weather belittled. The height above sea level, combined with the wind chill factor, can make mountain conditions similar to those experienced in Polar regions.

Key idea

Relatively low mountains are often more dangerous, simply because they are so underestimated.

Mountain survival will depend on your preparations, your kit and your mental attitude.

Preparations

If you know you are going to a mountain region, check the weather forecast in advance. Find out what the weather is usually like at the time of year you are going to be there. Although the weather is very changeable, there is no point exposing yourself to bad weather if you can avoid it. Knowing the likely weather will also assist in kit and clothing selection.

Remember this

You must advise someone of your route and estimated time of return. No one will be out looking for you unless they know you exist.

Upon arriving in the area, note the time the sun rises and sets. This will enable you to plan your daily itinerary and not be caught out in the dark. If forced to spend the night out, at least you will know how many hours you are going to tough it out for, and this may make survival more bearable.

Clothing

Your choice of clothing is extremely important. Mountain regions can expose you to high winds, sub-zero temperatures, snow and ice, and yet at higher altitudes, burn your face with powerful ultraviolet rays.

As you should know by now, the layering method of clothing is best. A core layer of thermals (e.g. Helly Hansen) are essential to draw away perspiration and to keep you dry. The second layer should be a loose-fitting shirt or polo neck top – something offering neck protection and buttoned or elasticated wrists. The third layer is a woollen jumper or fleece. The outer layer is a warm Gore-Tex waterproof. Don't neglect your legs: you need long-johns, waterproof over-trousers, and proper hiking socks. Keep clothing loose where you can, as it is the air inbetween the layers that insulates and keeps you warm. Avoid cotton where you can; its heat-retaining properties are minimal. Wool and man-made fibres are far superior and still help keep you warm if wet, unlike cotton.

Considerable heat is lost through the neck and head, simply because they are all too often uncovered. Wear a hat and scarf. Hoods and balaclavas do a good job, but you need a hard protective hat underneath in mountain regions, as falling rocks occur all the time. Gore-Tex type mittens should be worn over gloves to protect your hands from the risks of frostbite. Boots and gaiters need to be of good quality, and suitable for the foreseeable conditions. Lightweight fabric boots are not suitable in mountain areas where the cold and wet, as well as sharp rocks, will render most types inadequate. Poor footwear will slow you down and increase the chances of an accident.

At times, the hassle seems to outweigh the convenience, but you must stop periodically to put on or take off clothing. The weather and your body temperature change, and you must change with them. Too many of us soldier on, sweating buckets, rather than pausing for five minutes to take off a layer. Not only will this lead to dehydration, but your sweat-soaked body will cool dangerously when you stop, and you'll have hypothermia to contend with.

Suitable kit for mountains

Take a means of communicating with the outside world if an emergency arises. In many cases a mobile phone is ideal, but the cold reduces battery life, and the signal may be weak or non-existent in some mountain areas. Walkie-talkies may be better, but have quite a limited range of only a few miles. Check the area you are going to and ask professional guides, Mountain Rescue, or the local emergency services what devices will work. Torches (and spare batteries), flares and rescue whistles should be carried. Never rely on a visual method of signalling alone as low clouds make poor visibility commonplace.

Do not carry your map in the map pocket on the side of your trousers. Use a proper waterproof map case, and always have a spare map. Laminated maps are available for many areas and will last longer, and are less inclined to turn into a soggy papier-mâché mush. Carry a good compass, **and a spare.**

Each person should have their own waterproof bivvy bag and spare food to get them through an unexpected 24 hours on the hills. Liquids are unlikely to be a problem as you can suck snow or ice. However, do take something for the duration of the expected hike, but have regard to it freezing solid if unprotected and caught out in sub-zero conditions. A flask of sweet hot chocolate would be a bonus.

Since you will be above the tree-line, do not rely on finding firewood. If heating food is necessary, bring your own stove and prepare to use it in windy conditions.

Any kit such as Swiss army knives, compasses, torches, etc. should be attached to you by lanyards and/or straps. Drop something, and it could fall into an inaccessible crevice, or a hundred feet down, perhaps into deep snow.

Ice axes, ropes and harnesses should be carried, and you should know how to use them. It is well worth doing a short course in basic rock climbing and rope work. Mountaineering and rock climbing are dangerous, more so without proper training. Knowing how to abseil or climb out of trouble could be useful. An emergency is not a good time to practise something you read in a book a month ago.

Dangers

▶ Hypothermia

This is probably the main danger to contend with. It is where the body stops being able to generate heat, and unless you do something about it, death *will* follow. The usual cause is being wet and cold for too long, worsened by physical labour, e.g. hiking up and down mountains for hours on end!

Key idea

Common symptoms of hypothermia are irrational behaviour, fatigue with sudden bursts of energy, shivering, stumbling, headaches and confusion. The treatment is to get dry and warm as quickly as possible. Warm, sweet drinks will help. If shelter isn't available, you will be warmer moving, rather than sitting on a cold rock and allowing more heat to drain away. Replace wet clothing if possible.

▶ Broken bones

Twisted ankles, fractures and cuts are also common risks as falls, even small ones, can be serious. Customize your medical kit with falls in mind. Climbing helmets will reduce injury from falling rocks. More injuries occur descending, when you are tired, and prone to carelessness. Zig-zag going up and down, and it will reduce the strain on your knees and muscles. Avoid travelling after dark, it is too dangerous. A head torch is unlikely to shed enough light, or for long enough, to guarantee your safety.

▶ Avalanches

These are most common in the afternoons, more so during the warmer months. As the newer fresh snow melts, there is a chance it will slide off the harder frozen snow beneath, and cause an avalanche. If caught in its path, try to shield yourself behind rocky outcrops or trees. If not, try to get to the surface facing downhill as the snow tries to smoother you. You'll either have the time of your life, or die! Start burrowing your way out as soon as possible, as the cold will numb and paralyse you. A small emergency beacon to help mountain rescuers find you would be an excellent bit of kit to carry. Most climbing and outdoor equipment shops sell them.

Common indicators of being in avalanche-prone territory are:

▶ The hill is of a 30 to 50 degree slope.

▶ There are no bushes or trees to anchor the snow.

▶ The hillside is of a slightly convex shape.

▶ Fresh snow has fallen recently on the existing snow.

▶ It is getting warmer.

▶ Acute mountain sickness (AMS)

This affects around 40 per cent of us once we go higher than about 2500 metres. Symptoms are headaches, fatigue, weakness, dizziness and nausea. AMS is usually caused by ascending to the 2000-metre level too quickly. AMS itself is not life threatening, but it can be followed by cerebral or pulmonary oedema (an excessive build-up of fluid), and these can be fatal. The treatment is to deal with the headache (any painkiller should be taken), drink plenty and descend quickly. Small oxygen canisters and medicines such as Diamox should be put in your medical kit if high-altitude climbs/hikes are planned, as both can be life-savers if AMS deteriorates to an oedema. Speak to your usual doctor about supplies.

▶ Navigation errors

In the Scottish Highlands alone where the highest peak, Ben Nevis, is only 1344 metres there are dozens of deaths and serious injuries *every* year. Inexperienced navigators often rely too heavily on a GPS unit that fails them or runs out of batteries: they get lost, stumble and fall. Many get hypothermia because they end up spending longer on the hills than planned, and soon use up their supply of sufficient food and water. They become exhausted. The situation can be worsened if you underestimate the weather and bring inappropriate clothing. By all means take a GPS unit with you, but take a map as back-up. You must know how to navigate by using a traditional compass, as well as your GPS. If with others, ensure everyone knows the ascent route, where the safe places are to go in the event of a storm, and what route is to be taken on the descent.

▶ Temperature

Remember the temperature drops by two degrees for every 300 metres/1000 feet you ascend, and that doesn't take into account the wind chill factor. The wind chill factor means, at ground level, in a 20 mph wind at a tolerable minus 5°C, it can quickly become a biting minus 15 in minutes. As the wind picks up, and you ascend, the temperature will drop even further.

If you are wet, you act as a better conductor for heat loss, and can lose your body heat some 25 times faster than if dry but at the same temperature.

Case study

There are a great many survival stories involving the mountains. Many famous ascents of the Eiger, K2 and Everest have incredible tales of endurance and tragedy. My own attempt at the Eiger and a spell in the Venezuelan Andes were not without valuable lessons. However, the story of tough hockey player Eric LeMarque shows how easy it is for a harmless bit of recreation to turn into a life-threatening survival situation due to over-confidence and underestimating mountain conditions.

In February 2004, wearing only a light layer of clothing, LeMarque set out to snowboard the unmarked trails of the 11,000-feet Mammoth Mountain in California's Sierra Nevada mountain range.

A storm blew in and LeMarque became trapped on the mountain. He should have either spotted the early signs of the approaching storm and descended quickly, or at least telephoned and found out the weather conditions in advance. He was now stuck on the mountain. He initially tried to get to down, but became lost in the poor conditions and headed off in the wrong direction.

Temperatures were soon below zero, and LeMarque couldn't keep his wet feet warm. They became numb and discoloured. Frostbite was rapidly claiming them. He realized his weakness, and that he may not be as tough as he thought he was.

Using his snowboard like an axe, he chopped down some branches, and slept on top, and off, the heating-sapping snow. He used a plastic bag as a water container, and gathered snow in order to melt it.

Using the radio of his small MP3 player, he noticed the signal was far stronger if pointed it in one direction: he assumed this was the direction of the nearby town. In the absence of a compass, he reckoned the MP3 would work just as well as long as he headed in the direction of the strong signal. However he was not up to travelling now, and was cold, weak and very lost.

He found a point he believed rescuers could find, and decided to stay put. Rather than racing about in the mountain snow, he realized his best course of action was to conserve calories and heat, and sit tight.

He remembered how to dig snow caves from an ecology class, as well as how to use trees for protection. He dug himself a snow cave with his snowboard and then lined it with branches and bark to make it as dry as possible.

LeMarque believed his tough ice hockey training paid off, and gave him the strength to withstand considerable discomfort.

LeMarque's ordeal lasted far longer than he expected, or was equipped for. Two days became four, and then four became eight. During his eight days on the mountain, he had fallen into a freezing river and was swept over a waterfall. He was later forced to climb up an ice cliff, and spent his nights in fear of being attacked by wolves.

Eventually LeMarque was found. He had lost a considerable amount of weight, and his core body temperature had plummeted. The extensive frostbite to both his feet required amputation. But he was alive.

Mental attitude

Your chances of survival are greatly enhanced with a positive attitude. Visualize the end point and reaching safety. Stay calm, but determined. Panic burns more calories than you can probably spare, and usually results in the wrong decision being made.

When faced with a sudden disaster, initially pull back, stop doing anything, assess the situation and review your choices. Do not accept failure as an option. Be decisive in your actions, and remain focused on your objective. Keep together if in a team, and make sure everyone knows the plan.

British Special Forces train in the Black Mountains with good reason: trekking and climbing in mountain regions is *extremely* demanding, and often very hazardous. Don't be another accident statistic and someone else's lesson to learn from: research, anticipate, prepare, train – survive.

Focus points

* Do not underestimate mountain conditions.
* Many accidents and fatalities occur because of inadequate clothing, fatigue, low visibility or poor navigation.
* Check the weather forecast *before* you go.
* Wear and take proper outdoor clothing, don't cut corners.
* Let someone know where you are going and your estimated time of return.
* Test all equipment *before* you go.
* Consider enrolling in useful courses, such as mountain navigation, rope techniques and rock climbing.

Next step

You need to be able to travel without limits. Deaths in desert regions are often the result of navigation errors and underestimating the true nature of these vast empty places. Too many people perish through ignorance. You need to be able to extend your freedom and enjoy, rather than endure, these beautiful parts of the world.

21

Desert survival

In this chapter you will learn:

▶ *How to prioritize your survival needs*
▶ *How to reduce your fluid loss and recognize the signs of dehydration*
▶ *Where to look for water sources*
▶ *How to stay cool in the desert heat*
▶ *How to deal with snakes and scorpions*
▶ *What preparations to make before you go*

Desert survival is largely a matter of anticipation and preparation. However, by remaining calm and applying a little knowledge, you will increase your chances of survival even if you find yourself in a desert region ill-prepared and ill equipped.

As with mountain environments, too many people underestimate the temperature and weather in desert regions. The relatively featureless terrain can also mean that getting lost is all too easy. Having personally spent time in the desert regions on four continents, I find them fascinating places worthy of visits and exploration. You do need to plan ahead, and some specialist equipment will always help but, ultimately, survival is about your state of mind.

Immediate action

If your vehicle breaks down or your plane crash lands in a desert – stay with it. Your aircraft or vehicle is much easier for rescuers to see than a tiny figure (probably in sand-coloured clothing) wandering in thousands of square miles of desert. If you are on a regular route, staying on it will also increase your chances of being found by a passer-by sooner than later. Your vehicle/plane will also offer shade and protection from the elements – stay with it!

Once you have established shade, your next priority is to evaluate your situation and check your water rations. Have a clear plan of action before dehydration and the energy-sapping heat impair your ability to think straight.

In these situations you need to apply the STOP process to ensure you do not panic or overlook something crucial. First, Stop and do nothing for a moment. Think about your situation, what your priorities should be, and what are the immediate dangers that have to be dealt with. Observe your surroundings, yourself, and any other travellers with you. Only having first stopped, thought and observed can you now start to Plan, and decide how best to use your resources.

Case study

I had spent over a year preparing for my trip across the Sahara Desert, intending to reach Timbuktu on a motorcycle. I had completed a basic, then advanced, mechanics course, and also learned some basic Arabic. I honed my survival skills and tested every item of equipment thoroughly.

Despite my preparations things did not go smoothly. My travelling companion, a fellow motorcyclist and a far better mechanic than myself, decided the risks were too great and turned back. We were only two weeks into a trip expected to take three months. I continued alone, but then my motorbike broke down in the middle of nowhere, in the hottest part of the day.

I quickly assessed the problem, and decided the bike could be repaired. I put up my small tent, took a drink, and then rested in the shade for a few hours until it cooled down. When it was cool enough, but before it grew too dark, I started to repair the bike. Very methodically, I laid out the tools, and carefully put each removed part on a towel beside me. Eventually working by torch-light, I repaired the bike and put everything back together. I had taken repeated sips of water throughout the process. Once I felt everything was finished, I crawled back into the tent and slept until dawn.

Now fully rested, and after a further drink, I tested the bike in the morning light. All seemed well, and I was able to complete the next stage of my journey, and ultimately went on to reach my destination, Timbuktu, safely.

Accurate navigation had been necessary at every stage as the desert winds quickly hid any tracks I started to use. I had also been aware of the possible magnetic effect of the bike's components on the compass, and the effect that even slight dehydration would have on my attitude and behaviour. I was later told that one in five travellers perished crossing the Sahara.

Water

To survive on low water rations, you must first reduce body fluid loss. Help yourself by doing the following:

► Stay fully clothed. The body sweats as a means of staying cool as the slow evaporation of sweat from the skin produces a life-saving cooling effect. You accelerate the evaporation of sweat by being uncovered and don't give the skin the benefit of the cooling effect. The body responds by continually producing more sweat. Valuable loss of fluid like this is dangerous and avoidable – stay covered up! Reduce the need to sweat by staying clothed.

► Dampen clothes with undrinkable liquids (or urine) to keep yourself cool and reduce the need to sweat in the first place.

► Eat less, and stop drinking alcohol and smoking.

► Rest in the day and work/walk only when the air temperature cools – if it is safe to do so.

► Suck a button or pebble to relieve the feeling of thirst.

► Avoid talking, and try not to breathe through your mouth, as water (in vapour form) is lost every time you open your mouth. Breathe through your nose if you can.

Without drinking water and resting in the shade, you will last only two to three days in temperatures of 50°C. Drink sparingly as excess water cannot be stored and will be excreted out and wasted.

Before water runs low and *before* you are too weak or dehydrated, start looking for more. Try:

► Digging at the lowest part of the outside bend of a dry riverbed.

► Digging at natural low spots where water might gather.

► Covering any plants with plastic and collecting water that accumulates by condensation.

► Draining your vehicle's radiator – unless it contains antifreeze.

► Making **several** solar stills. Dig a hole one metre deep by one metre wide. Place a container in the bottom. Cover the hole with a plastic sheet and seal the edges of it with stones and sand so moisture in the hole cannot escape. Drop a weight in the middle of the sheet, directly above your container. Water will collect on the underside of the plastic sheet, run down the sides and drip into your container. You can put any vegetation, damp clothes, etc, in the hole to boost the production of water.

> If you find damp ground, soak up moisture with a cloth, then wring it out into a container. Physical work should be done during the coolest part of the day. Always balance water loss (perspiration) against the likely water gain.

Remember this

Do not rely on one method of water procurement alone; have several solar stills on the go, while looking for water by other means.

Key idea

Dehydration often goes unnoticed until you are incapacitated. Common symptoms include dark-coloured urine, headaches, ringing in your ears, irritability, indecisiveness, loss of appetite and fatigue. Although dehydration is a killer in its own right, it more often leads to errors in judgement which themselves cause disasters.

Case study

In 2012, South African Mauritz Pieterse, aged 25, and Josh Hayes, aged 30, were in the Australian desert when their four-wheel drive became stuck in soft sand. They were both experienced in travelling through the area, as they were working for the National Reserve and were familiar with working outdoors. Certain basic survival rules should have kicked in but regrettably did not.

They could not free their vehicle, so (wrongly) decided to try and walk back to a farm they thought they passed about ten miles back. They carried only a small amount of water when they chose to leave the vehicle and walk. It was in the afternoon, and the temperature was in excess of 40°C.

A rescuer found Pieterse's body on a bush track later that evening. It had taken only hours of dehydration and exhaustion to kill him.

The rescuer later found Hayes too, lying under a bush and barely alive. He believed that had he been left unfound for another hour or so, he too would have died. Hayes was not even wearing a hat against the sun. He was described as having wide owl-like eyes, sunk into his head. Once cooled down, rehydrated, and given medical attention, he made a full recovery.

Staying cool

Use your vehicle to create a cool, shaded area where you can rest. Avoid lying or sitting directly on hot surfaces. Rig up an awning from anything you can find, as metal aeroplanes and vehicles will heat up in the sun, and sitting in them will be like sitting in an oven.

If you have no vehicle to adapt, cover up and create shade as best you can. Consider digging a trench and lying in the shade it creates; use any towels, items of clothing or a tent/poncho as a shield against the heat and the sun.

Wear light, baggy clothing and cover yourself completely. Clothing acts as a shield against the sun's rays to a large extent and stops hot rays heating you up. Staying covered up also reduces the likelihood of sunburn.

Wear boots. Exposed feet, even in sandals, are at the mercy of the sun as well as insects, scorpions and snakes. Keep clothing and boots loose to allow for the circulation of air. Lighter-coloured clothing will reflect heat away better than darker-coloured clothing.

Eating generates heat as the food is broken down. Eating should therefore be limited to the cooler parts of the day and only if you have adequate water. The process of digestion requires considerable amounts of liquid. If you eat without drinking enough water, you will worsen the effects of dehydration and not be doing yourself any favours.

Some common problems

Glare: The continual glare from the sun is fatiguing and causes discomfort and headaches. Sunglasses reduce the likelihood of sand or grit blowing into your eyes. If you do not have any sunglasses, improvise. Make a bandit-style mask with thin slits for your eyes from whatever you can find. Blackening the area around your eyes with soot/charcoal will also help.

Disorientation: Deserts are notoriously easy to get lost in. There are often no discernible landmarks, tracks blow away in sand storms, and human occupation is minimal. Take accurate navigation very seriously; errors could easily result in your running out of fuel and water prematurely.

Heatstroke (Hyperthermia): This is when the body loses the ability to control its temperature. Sweating stops and the skin becomes hot and dry. The usual dehydration symptoms are present but dizziness progresses to delirium, then to unconsciousness, and ultimately to death. Treatment is by cooling the body by either immersing in tepid water (cold water may induce a heart attack), or by wetting the clothes, fanning and resting in the shade. Drink what you can and massage the limbs to maintain blood flow. Being in a waterless desert makes treatment very difficult, so prevention is paramount.

Snakes and scorpions: Many are heat seeking, and I vividly recall my morning brews over a small hexamine stove in the Sahara regularly attracting half a dozen scorpions. Resting directly on the sand can be risky. Avoid rocky places too. Wear proper boots and long trousers as most snake bites are below the knee.

Carry a venom extractor and anti-venom if possible. Since evacuation to a hospital is unlikely to be an option you will have to treat yourself in situ. Wrap a tight bandage (but not a tourniquet) above the bite site, working your way down and over it. Stay calm and cool yourself as much as possible. The idea is to slow the rate of the poison spreading and to give your lymphatic system a chance to tackle it. Ice or something cold, will ease the pain. Take comfort in the fact that few bites and stings are fatal to healthy adults. I met a fellow traveller while in the Negev Desert who had suffered several snake bites and treated scorpion bites as being like irritating bee stings.

Preparations

If you expect to go through or over a desert region, consider taking the following:

▶ A medical kit customized to dealing with dehydration and heat-related conditions. Cuts quickly become infected in the heat, so bring antiseptics and wide-spectrum antibiotics. The continual sand and dust can also give rise to throat and eye infections, so bring appropriate medications. I took three courses of antibiotics on a trip to the Gobi Desert and ended up using them all.

▶ Water filters and sterilizing tablets, as well as adequate containers to fill up at watering points. Water bags rather than bulky water bottles are often easier to carry.

▶ Flares, heliographs, emergency rescue beacons, and a pre-arranged rescue plan if you don't get to a point by a certain date.

▶ Sunblock (and burn treatment cream), a hat and sunglasses.

▶ GPS (and spare batteries) compass and map, and spares of each.

▶ Sun-proof flysheet or tarpaulin.

 Try it now

Acclimatize to the heat if you can before you go. Try saunas to ensure the sweat glands are fully functioning before exposing yourself to the heat. The risk of many heat-related conditions is lessened by gradual adaptation rather than sudden exposure.

Your chances of survival generally will be greater if you are less reliant on others and become your own mechanic, medic, navigator, linguist, etc. Invest in yourself and extend your freedom.

Focus points

✳ Stay with your vehicle/aircraft if you break down or crash land in a desert.

✳ Reduce your fluid loss by walking and working after sundown, and breathing through your nose, not your mouth.

✳ Wet your clothes in undrinkable water or urine to stay cool.

✳ Be precise in your navigation, as the lack of landmarks can make getting lost all too easy.

Next step

The final environment to prepare for is the Polar regions, primarily the Arctic. The Arctic Circle includes parts of Scandinavia, Canada and Russia, and is therefore more likely to be visited than Antarctica in the south. Unlike Antarctica, there is no permanent land mass but there are more types of animals including polar bears and wolves.

22

Arctic survival

In this chapter you will learn:

- ► *How to better understand Arctic conditions*
- ► *How to prioritize your needs in an emergency*
- ► *How to build a shelter*
- ► *How to navigate if your compass is lost*
- ► *Where to find food and fresh water sources*
- ► *How to stay warm, and how best to travel*

There is nothing like sub-zero temperatures, week-long blizzards, and inadequate food and fuel to test your resilience! The Arctic Circle covers an area that includes parts of Sweden, Finland and Norway, but also parts of Canada, Russia and Greenland. With an increasing number of expeditions and travel opportunities to venture within the Arctic Circle, perhaps it's time you prepared for, and understood, this unforgiving place a little better.

The conditions

Arctic summers are around 18°C, and winters are around minus 55°C. Altitude and wind will lower temperatures even further. A wind of only 20 mph will make an uncomfortable minus 14°C feel like an unbearable minus 25°C. When I was in Siberia, some areas had recorded temperatures of minus 70°C! If it's any consolation, Antarctica in the south is even colder. Exposed skin will freeze pretty quickly at these temperatures.

Apart from the cold, the white-out conditions and featureless terrain make navigation and travel difficult. Magnetic compasses are too close to the Pole to be relied upon. Although the wider Arctic Circle does have animals and plants on the land, the actual Pole and surrounding area are just ice. The waters have seals and fish beneath the ice, if you can get to them. With little accessible animal or plant life, all food and fuel has to be carried. Do not fool yourself into thinking you can easily live off the land if your own supplies run low.

Do remember that, during the summer, much of the Arctic Circle which encompasses land is over-populated with biting insects such as mosquitoes. At times there are ten times more mosquitoes in the Arctic than in the tropics.

Remember this

Pack plenty of repellent to protect your face, which is often the only exposed skin and attracts thousands of blood-seeking insects. Although the insects do not carry malaria, and there is a low risk of infection in the Arctic, the insects can cause distractions and irritability which may lead to dangerous errors.

Many environments, including the Arctic, are unforgiving: if you are not prepared and get sloppy, you will suffer and you will die.

Immediate action

The cold will quickly dull your mind and drain you of energy: you must act while you can. Your immediate concerns are to:

▶ Take shelter and get out of the cold and wind.

▶ Send an SOS, and/or have a means of signalling ready once rescuers get close by. Burn something that will produce dark smoke to contrast the white background: spare tyres, or anything containing rubber or plastic is good.

▶ Attend to any wounds or medical matters.

▶ Assess your food, water and fuel supplies.

▶ Try to calculate where you are, and whether it is worth waiting for help, or trying to reach a nearby settlement. Take into account weather conditions, food supplies and the physical condition of you and anyone with you.

Shelter

You must get out of the wind – try to create a small enclosure. Erect a tent, poncho, or perhaps get more comfortable in your broken down vehicle. In high winds, or if you are without a shelter, you must use the snow. Dig with whatever you have, and make a trench. Peg out or weigh down a poncho to cover it, and crawl underneath (see Figure 22.1). Or, dig a hole or cave into the side of a snow drift, making the entrance smaller once you're inside.

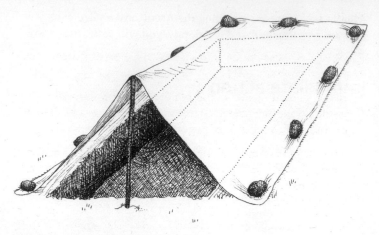

Figure 22.1 A trench shelter (© Kate Polley)

Try it now

As an exercise, and before you need to do so, make yourself a trench shelter in the snow, and see how deep and wide you need to dig, and what a night in it is really like. This will better prepare you if a genuine survival situation arises, and will take away some of the shock and uncertainty if you suddenly find yourself having to spend the night out ill-prepared.

Another shelter to consider building is a moulded dome shelter. Pile your pack and equipment in one place and drape over a tarp or poncho. Now cover with snow, leaving a small door on one side. Pack the snow down and leave for a few hours for it to freeze tight. Once you are satisfied it has hardened, carefully remove the kit piece by piece through the door, and crawl inside.

Building an igloo out of blocks of ice is unrealistic unless you have a snow/ ice saw, and have practised making one in less life-threatening circumstances, preferably with expert tuition.

Shelter building in the Arctic can be made easier if you have in mind the following:

▶ Never lay tools on the snow. They will soon disappear and worsen your situation.

▶ Avoid generating sweat and remove a layer or two while you work. Sweat may freeze once you stop moving, and thereby expose you to the risk of hypothermia.

▶ Keep shelters simple and use any natural features and materials where possible. Valuable calories spent building an elaborate shelter may not be recoverable. Insufficient calories will make you cold, fatigued, and a burden to yourself and others.

▶ Use simple knots as your numb fingers may not be able to undo sophisticated knots in thin cord.

▶ Ensure your shelter has ventilation. The build up of dangerous gases, particularly if using a stove, can lead to asphyxiation – you'll simply die in your sleep.

▶ Minimize contact with the ground by laying out an insulating mat, a carpet of small sticks, or even a poncho with some soft kit underneath.

▶ Ensure the prevailing wind does not blow straight into the entrance of your shelter.

Staying warm

Obviously, suitable clothing is essential, and the following will help further:

▶ Clothing should be fairly loose, as trapped air is superb insulation.

▶ Ensure you have adequate ventilation by having cuffs and collars that can be loosened if need be.

Key idea

If you start to generate sweat, it may cool you down too much when you stop moving, and thereby increase the risk of hypothermia, so stay vigilant and try not to sweat.

- Concentrate on staying dry inside and out. Damp clothing will cool you down very quickly, perhaps dangerously so. Brush snow off you before it melts and seeps through to your skin.

- Wearing several thin layers is better than one or two very thick ones. The trapped air warms up and insulates you. Also, wearing several layers enables you to regulate your temperature by allowing you to put on or take off additional layers.

- Your outer jacket must be Gore-Tex or similar. Purely waterproof clothing tends to allow body vapour to build up, and leaves clothes damp.

- Unless you are engaged in potentially sweat-producing physical work, reduce body heat loss by having a draw-string around your middle, and tightened cuffs. Improvise with a piece of cord if need be.

- Clothing should be of the right materials. Wool does not readily absorb water, and will therefore keep you dry if wet. Cotton is a killer and soaks up moisture too easily. Many synthetic materials are purpose-made for the job and keep you warm and dry when you most need it. Choose your clothing carefully, your life may depend on it.

- Wear several pairs of socks, ensuring your boots are large enough to still be comfortable. Be careful of restricting blood flow by tying laces too tight. Gaiters are a must.

- Wear gloves under a larger and waterproof (or Gore-Tex) mitten. Mittens are much warmer than gloves, and wearing a combination of the two is preferred. Keep them on a cord so they aren't lost if you remove them to do a fiddly job.

 Try it now

Reassess your clothing. Tie gloves and mittens together. Attach larger zip pulls to small zip fasteners, and review the suitability of anything with small fiddly buttons, made of 100 per cent cotton, or perhaps simply too well fitting.

Case study

In 1912 the *Saint Anna* was on an exploratory expedition under Captain Georgiy Brusilov. They had set off from what is now called Murmansk, a coastal city in northern Russia on the Barents Sea. The plan was to emerge at the other end of the North-east Passage at Vladivostok, and also see if the area was a viable Arctic hunting ground.

Brusilov was criticized from the start as being ill-prepared and incompetent. The crew were not particularly experienced either, and food supplies were limited – and low in vitamin C. Scurvy and starvation would be real risks if the trip overran – which an experienced explorer would know to prepare for. Having no contingency plan is unwise in remote areas where rescue is unlikely.

The ship did not leave port until late in the year, which meant it was likely they would have to deal with the Arctic pack ice. Less than two months into the expedition, the *Saint Anna* did indeed become trapped in the ice. Although they were close enough to Siberia, and could have left the ship, the Captain decided that staying on board until the ice melted in the forthcoming warmer summer months was the better option.

However, the pack ice pulled the ship further and further north, and it was not freed as the Captain had expected. They were now thousands of miles off course, and supplies were running dangerously low. Scurvy had immobilized several members of the crew, and fuel had all but been used up. They had been gone around 18 months at this stage, and without resupply, or rescue, were clearly going to die.

The navigation officer, Valerian Albanov, had been critical of the captain for months. Albanov felt that death was a question of 'when' and not 'if' and he would need to leave the ship if he were to survive. He believed that his best hope of survival was to reach Franz Josef Land, which he knew lay somewhere to the south. Unfortunately, the only map he had of this relatively unknown area was in a 20-year-old travel book. Franz Josef Land was simply indicated by dotted lines.

In January 1914, Albanov and 13 crew members decided to act rather than wait for death. They built themselves some kayaks and sledges and, with the captain's consent, abandoned the *Saint Anna*. Three turned back after only a few days. Albanov started to keep a diary, which was later published. It makes for gripping reading.

They planned to try and reach Cape Flora on Franz Josef Land, where they believed there were cabins and supplies from a former expedition. It was over 200 miles away. Albanov had no accurate way to determine longitude, and he had to guess and use his intuition as to where Franz Josef Land lay.

They had to cope with continuous shifting ice, attacks by polar bears and walrus, as well as dealing with disintegrating ice floes, blizzards, snow-blindness and, inevitably, a lack of food. However, Albanov came into his own, as if he had been waiting his whole life for such a challenge, and he shone as a natural leader. He convinced his men to continue dragging the homemade kayaks on their homemade sledges, even though they were energy-sapping and heavy. Albanov realized that without the kayaks they would not survive in the constantly moving ice-bound waters around the Franz Josef archipelago.

They finally sighted land, but getting onto it was still a major problem. To add to Albanov's difficulty, two of the weary crew slipped away in the night, stealing some of the team's supplies and equipment. Then, within almost touching distance of the land, a storm blew the unstable ice floes apart, and the small team of desperate survivors were temporarily separated from one another.

The men were later reunited, and managed to climb up a glacier – with their sledges and kayaks – and at last walked onto solid land. Finding food was a priority. They came across some eider ducks, and raided their nests for the eggs.

While hunting, Albanov then stumbled upon the two men who had slipped away in the night. However, by this time he was forgiving, and overcome with emotion. He decided to pardon them, rather than punish them; executing them for mutiny was the expected response.

The exhausted party continued to head towards Cape Flora on Franz Josef Land, hoping to find the old cabins, and perhaps supplies, left behind by the previous expedition many years before them. Progress was painful, and scurvy killed one man and severely incapacitated three others. The team divided into two: four would travel with sledges by land, while the other five, including Albanov, would travel in the two kayaks. As they had been unable to catch a large mammal for food, they were reduced to eating raw ducks, which they shot with their rifles.

Despite these hardships, Albanov maintained his diary. It shows his strength, and that he was not a beaten man. He tried to plan ahead, create contingency plans, and generally stay positive but realistic.

By now the sledges were falling apart, and were effectively just fragments and splinters held together with bits of wire and string. Their clothes were dirty rags soaked in seal oil and alive with lice.

The kayakers decided to keep moving when the sledge party did not meet up with them at a pre-arranged rendezvous point. Albanov knew they would perish if they did not reach the old expedition camp soon, and continued onward. As if to test them further, another storm separated the two kayaks. Albanov and his companion, Alexander Konrad, were forced to wait out the storm. By doing so, they lost contact with the three men in the other kayak. Albanov and Konrad nearly drowned while sleeping, when the iceberg they were sheltering on started to disintegrate, but miraculously the men managed to sum up enough strength to crawl back into their kayak, and paddle back to Bell Island, the closest land. Days later, Albanov and Konrad reached the old camp. The cabins *were* still standing, and did have some old, but useable, supplies left behind.

Albanov and Konrad realized they were the sole survivors and prepared to spend the winter at Cape Flora. They spent time improving the cabin, and replenishing it with all the supplies they could find. Then, quite unexpectedly, a ship appeared and the two men were rescued.

It had been three months since they had left the *Saint Anna*. No trace of any of the other men, or of the *Saint Anna* itself, has ever been found. In 2010, a Russian expedition followed the route of the *Saint Anna* and found a human skeleton, a watch, snowshoes, a knife, and a spoon marked with a sailor's initials, all on the shores of Franz Josef Land.

The full story of this struggle in the Arctic is found in Albanov's own diaries, published as *In the Land of White Death*.

Food and water

The Arctic offers little plant life to keep a starved survivor alive. You need around 5,000 calories a day to enable you to travel and move about in Arctic temperatures, often more. While there are edible plants on the tundra, they cannot fulfil your calorific needs. You need meat.

Fish, seals, foxes, rabbits, caribou, and even several types of bear, frequent the Arctic and can be trapped, shot, clubbed or speared. Many birds such as ptarmigan and owl are relatively tame, and with slow movements you may get close enough to catch them. Raid any nests you find for eggs.

Once caught, gut your prey before the flesh freezes and makes cutting too difficult. Cut the flesh into blocks of meat to make cooking, and perhaps carrying it, that much easier.

Key idea

Avoid eating the livers of polar animals, particularly seals and bears, as they often have dangerously high levels of vitamin A. The liver should be easy to identify as the large, dark red, organ not too far below the rib cage.

Water should not be a problem, but be aware that fresh, clear sea ice will have a high salt content, and should therefore be avoided. The darker and older sea ice will be safer. Test it before gathering it up to melt as drinking water. Also be aware that the snow itself may be contaminated with salt water spray, so gather any snow you intend to melt down for drinking, away from the sea.

Remember this

Never eat snow or ice directly. In sub-zero Arctic conditions, it may damage the skin around your mouth. It will also worsen both hypothermia and dehydration. Compress snow and suck it like an ice lolly, or simply melt it down.

Key idea

Address your food and water needs while you still have the strength to do so. Don't put it off until you are desperate, as by then you may be too weak to help yourself.

Travel

Being so close to the magnetic North Pole makes compasses unreliable without complicated calculations. Unless you are geared up to do the necessary calculations, or precise navigation is not called for, a more reliable navigational aid will be the stars or a GPS unit. However, during Arctic summers, the sun does not set properly at night, and stars are barely visible as a consequence. The 'shadow tip' method of direction finding could therefore be useful – see 'Try it now' below.

Try it now

Put a one metre high stick into the snow. Mark the point where the shadow tip ends with something. Wait at least 20 minutes, but longer if you can. Mark the shadow tip again. Remove the stick and lay it between the two markers. The first one indicates west, the second east. North and south can be found quite easily now.

This method of direction finding is mentioned more than once in this book, because it is simple and effective. Practise it, before your life depends on it.

Deep crevices, ice-cold water, frozen rivers and snow several metres deep making hiking on foot virtually impossible. Skis and/ or snow shoes are vital. You *must* bring some with you. Making some improvised ones if you are without them is unrealistic. Do not venture into the Arctic thinking you will make some skis or snow shoes if the need arises. Even if you had practised making them previously, doing so under life-threatening survival conditions is very difficult and largely impractical.

I spent nearly a year in the Arctic, and must stress the need to be prepared and to plan ahead, more so than for any other environment. Undoing a button or re-tying a boot lace is a major task at minus 50°C! Keep all food and kit in easy to open bags and containers.

Remember this
Think ahead: if you fail to plan, plan to fail.

Conditions such as frost bite and hypothermia are covered in Chapter 24 in which we discuss how to deal with the cold generally.

Focus points
* The extreme cold paralyses the mind and the body, so quick and decisive action is needed before you lose too much control.
* Try to stay as dry as possible, as you lose body heat much quicker if wet.
* You need two to three times more calories in Arctic conditions.
* Be practical in the kind of shelter you attempt to build; snow holes and trenches are more realistic and less calorie-sapping than intricate and energy-demanding igloos.

Next step
Two of the most common killers in the outdoors, particularly to those engaged in outdoor pursuits, are the cold and the heat. Both are all too often underestimated, and both claim lives as a result of travellers being unaware and under-prepared. We will start with gaining a better understanding of the lethal effects of the heat.

23

The heat

In this chapter you will learn:

▶ *What kind of clothing to wear in hot conditions*

▶ *About the best method of travel in the heat*

▶ *How to conserve body fluids and thereby reduce your fluid needs*

▶ *How to treat common heat-related medical conditions*

▶ *What preparations you should make before going to a hot climate*

The heat can kill. It can cause dehydration, heatstroke, severe cramps and blistering to the skin. More commonly, heat causes irritability and impairs your judgement, which themselves can cause otherwise avoidable accidents and wrong decisions.

It is important that you prepare yourself for the heat as you would any unfamiliar environment – do not just undo another shirt button and roll your sleeves up! You must raise your level of awareness and acknowledge that the effects of heat could be life threatening.

Clothing

Wearing the appropriate clothing is extremely important in the heat, just as it is in the cold. You don't see desert peoples in shorts and T-shirts with good reason – think of a typical Arab's clothing. You must protect yourself against sunburn, heat and insects. The general rules are:

▶ To reduce sunburn and fluid loss through evaporation, cover your whole body including arms and legs. Clothing damp with sweat also aids cooling. For this reason, shorts and T-shirts are inadvisable in the extreme heat.

▶ Wear loose, cotton clothing which is much cooler and more comfortable than tight fitting synthetic clothing, such as polyester.

▶ Light-coloured clothing is cooler as it reflects away the sun's rays more than dark-coloured clothing, which tends to absorb it.

▶ Always cover your head and neck. The head-dresses worn in the Middle East and Arabic countries, known as shemagh or keffiyeh, are not fashion accessories, they protect vital body parts from overheating and sunburn. As with clothing generally, using a light-coloured, cotton material is cooler.

Ignore these basic guidelines and you will dehydrate faster and will be more likely to suffer from heatstroke, sunburn and prickly heat.

Eye protection should not be ignored as squinting into a bright, blazing sun for hours on end will cause headaches, fatigue and considerable discomfort. Wear tinted goggles or sunglasses where possible. If need be, in extreme conditions, you can reduce the glare by blackening the area around your eyes with charcoal, or by making a make-shift mask with small slits for the eyes.

I find leather boots more comfortable than heavily padded, man-made fibre boots. Even the breathable fabrics don't seem to be cooler than a decent leather boot. Depending on your circumstances and likely activity (e.g. hiking) you may need to wear tough boots anyway.

If you need to remove clothing at all, do so in the shade and out of the sun. By all means dampen your clothing, but do so with undrinkable water (sea-water or urine for example), unless drinking water is in plentiful supply.

Apply sunblock to your face or, if without it, cover up as best you can. Again, think of how Arabs and desert people cover themselves.

Case study

I was in Nicaragua exploring the Mosquito Coast. It was July and it was hot and humid. I was hiking to an area my map said looked interesting, a round trip of about 20 miles. I had little with me, but several litres of bottled water and small medical kit. I wore ill-fitting, baggy clothes and a crumpled fishing hat. I had told the guest house where I was going and what time I should be back. I bought a few bags of crisps for lunch.

Several hours later, and now in a remote area miles from the town, I came across a Dutch couple who were sitting by the side of the footpath I was following. They were wearing colourful T-shirts, shorts and 'off-road' sandals. Insects buzzed around them angrily, and the man looked like death. His frantic girlfriend did not know what to do. Apparently her boyfriend had suffered cramps in his leg, fallen and injured his knee and shoulder. Their only water supplies were in the small rucksack he was wearing, and the container had burst during the fall, leaving them with nothing. They did not have a first aid kit, and the girl did not feel she could leave her boyfriend and go off for help.

They were both suffering from dehydration, and I had to surrender most of my water to help them recover. They also seemed to have heat exhaustion, so I gave them both a bag of salty crisps to help address the cramps and salt depletion. They needed to be cooled down, and so I moved them into the shade. first aid needed to be administered to the man, who had badly twisted his knee; his shoulder injury was not serious, just bruised and grazed.

After binding the man's knee with my bandana, I managed to get him up and hobbling. Between us, the girl and I supported him, and headed back to the town. With frequent stops, and lots of water, they made it back. Cool showers, more water, and rest were all the girl required to make a complete recovery. Her boyfriend did need to see a doctor about his knee, but otherwise recovered fully once cooled down and rehydrated. My own hike had to be postponed until another time. The incident heightened my awareness of how a short trip can suddenly turn into something very serious if a few basic rules are ignored.

Travel

Key idea

Avoid any walking or strenuous work between 11 am and 4 pm, the hottest part of the day.

Any physical activity in the heat should be limited. If possible, travel only in the evening or in the very early morning. Rest up in a shaded shelter during the day, taking care not to lie or sit on hot surfaces.

If travel in the heat is unavoidable, reduce the effort by avoid having to pass over steep or rough terrain if you can. Have a well-prepared route and try to minimize the amount of decision making, navigation and calculations you have to make once on the move. The effects of even mild dehydration, coupled with fatigue can cause you to make silly (and costly) mistakes.

Carry adequate water and plan ahead so you know where you can be resupplied. Leave nothing to chance – water is your lifeline to survival in the heat. It cools, it hydrates, it cleans.

Food and water

As water is required for digestion, you can eat yourself into a state of dehydration if you are not careful. If you are down to about half a litre a day, it is best to eat nothing. Foods that contain protein and/or fats require more water to digest them than other foods. Consequently, stick to carbohydrates where possible, at least until water is in plentiful supply.

Survival in the heat is about getting enough water into your system, but also about trying to conserve what fluids your body already has. You can reduce body fluid loss by:

▶ Staying fully clothed to reduce fluid loss through evaporation.

▶ Reducing perspiration, e.g. by limiting physical activity during the day.

▶ Resting in the shade where possible.

▶ Avoiding alcohol.

▶ Not smoking.

▶ Not talking – water vapour is lost every time you open your mouth.

▶ Avoiding lying or sitting on warm rocks or surfaces.

▶ Eating only if water is available.

The actual amount of water you need daily will depend on what you are doing, whether you can get out of the sun for any length of time, and whether you have any food or water at all. Ideally you ought to rest in the shade, drinking several litres a day, and only hike or undergo physical work early in the morning (before about 11 am) and again after about 4 pm when it is cooler.

Risks

Reduced amounts of salt and water (both lost through sweating) can cause several unpleasant conditions. Replace them where you can and be aware of your needs.

Heat cramps normally affect the limbs and abdomen and can be avoided by taking small amounts of salt daily, together with adequate water. The odd bag of salty crisps could be good for you after all! Salt tablets are also available from your doctor or chemist, and ought to be considered if travelling in a hot climate, more so if travelling to a remote area where resupply with the right kind of food and/or water may be difficult.

Heat exhaustion is also brought on by salt and water deficiencies both lost through excessive perspiration. You feel clammy, dizzy, get headaches and lose your appetite. You feel rotten. You need to drink (lots) and lie down in a cool shaded place. Elevate your legs to ensure adequate blood supply to your heart. Heat exhaustion can kill: take it seriously.

Heatstroke is slightly different but can also be fatal. This is the opposite of hypothermia in that this time the body loses the ability to cool down. You feel hot, dizzy, have headaches and may drift into delirium. You have to lower your body temperature quickly. Remove your clothing, stand in a breeze or fan, sprinkle yourself with cold water. Massaging your limbs will help to stimulate the circulation. Avoid drinking any stimulants (e.g., alcohol, coffee). Your aim is to get your body temperature down and then address any dehydration.

Dehydration is serious and very common. It can easily go undetected until quite advanced as thirst is a very unreliable indicator of your actual fluid needs. You lose literally litres of liquid each day through evaporation, sweat and urinating. You must drink regularly and not just when you feel thirsty.

Common symptoms include dark urine, headaches, ringing in your ears, a sense of irritation and a loss of appetite. Rehydration is improved quicker by drinking sweetened drinks; if you only have water add a spoon or two of sugar per cup. A pinch of salt per cup is also of benefit and will help counter cramps and heat exhaustion.

Prickly heat is intense itching, often around the groin area. It is where the sweat glands haven't yet adjusted to the change in heat and humidity, and get blocked. Wear loose clothing, preferably of non-synthetic material. Talc helps. Treat as an allergy and avoid using soap on the affected areas.

Sunburn should be avoided if you keep covered up and wear sunblock. Do not burst blisters as this will expose you to infection. Cool with wet cloths and then cover with a dry dressing to protect against further heat or rubbing. Traditional remedies such as calamine lotion will help, but prevention is better than a cure.

Insects and reptiles are more prevalent and dangerous in hot climates than in cold ones. Ants, centipedes, spiders and scorpions can all deliver nasty bites and commonly hide under rocks. Be careful if sitting down or if you need to move stones or rocks. Brush any insect or spider off you in the direction in which it is moving; it is easier to dislodge and is less likely to take defensive action.

Lizards and snakes normally bite below the knee, so wearing adequate boots and trousers will help. Pound the ground with heavy steps or a stick to scare them off if entering 'snake country'.

Studies show that mosquitoes and many other flying insects, such as bees, are actually attracted to the carbon dioxide you exhale. Try covering your mouth or holding your breath until out of range. Others are attracted to your sweat and body heat. Cover yourself up (particularly your head) and smother your clothing with repellent. Insects carry a wide range of unpleasant diseases including malaria, typhus and yellow fever. Maintain a high standard of hygiene as infections and disease spread rapidly in the heat.

Preparation

The discomfort produced by the heat can be adjusted to, and gradual acclimation is always recommended. While this is not always an option, the use of saunas leading up to the day of departure will help prepare you for the sudden heat and humidity as you get off the plane. Perhaps even try running and circuit training wearing more than normal, just to get you used to the heat and get the sweat glands up and running. Tanning shops and sun beds allow for gradual tanning weeks before you depart. These can also prepare the skin for the intense sun, and hopefully accelerate your protection. They will help prepare your skin for the sudden high intensity UV rays when you arrive.

Remember this

If you know where you are going, check the weather before you leave. This will allow you to bring suitable clothing and other kit. You may have underestimated the conditions. Try some weather websites such as www. metoffice.gov.uk or www.intellicast.com for round-the-world weather data and forecasts.

Pack enough water containers and verify where water can be obtained from, and whether it will need treating/purifying before drinking. If so, or if uncertain, bring purification tablets and filters. Do not leave your wellbeing to chance, or to someone else to protect.

Remember this

Customize your medical kit to address the risks above, together with plenty of painkillers, packs of sugar and some salt. Several packs of rehydration sachets are a must. Cuts and scratches can become quickly infected in the heat and humidity. Pack dressings, sterile cleaners and antiseptic creams. Sunblock, burns cream and lip protector will be useful, as will some sunglasses.

Carry a survival kit suitable for the climate and foreseeable conditions. Taking out the fishing kit, for example, might be a good idea if travelling through a desert.

The heat generally slows us down. It is nature's way of trying to preserve us by making us do less and so sweat less. Listen to your body and do not try to fight it: go with it and you'll live longer.

Focus points

* Loose fitting cotton clothing will keep you cool and protected from the sun's harmful UV rays.
* The heat can make us irritable and sloppy, and this may cause life-threatening accidents and wrong decisions.
* Reduce food intake if water is low. Digestion requires water, so you risk worsening dehydration.
* Have salt with your food in hot climates; it will help counter the effects of heat related medical conditions like cramps.

Next step

The cold is the other common killer and can affect us even if the environment we are in is not that cold. If we are wet, our temperature drops much faster than if we are dry. Hunger and exhaustion also accelerate a fall in our temperature. You need to heighten your awareness of the risks and do all you can to stay warm.

24

The cold

In this chapter you will learn:

▶ *The importance of eating and drinking enough in cold conditions*
▶ *How to find out the likely weather ahead*
▶ *What kind of clothes to wear and how to wear them*
▶ *How to accelerate your adaptation to the cold*
▶ *About common medical conditions brought on by the cold and how to treat them*

The cold is never far away and is not something only to take into account over the winter period. Desert temperatures can drop below zero at night and hiking in the spring rains can induce hypothermia. While the cold can kill and cripple in its own right, like the heat, it is more often the effects of the cold that lead to errors in judgement and fatal accidents.

The science

To stay warm you need to burn calories. The average male requires around 2,500 calories to stay warm and functional; in very cold conditions you should consider doubling this, and in Arctic conditions tripling it. Food is fuel, and will keep you warm. Watch your calorie intake, as hypothermia is never far behind hunger.

Blood carries heat around the body. In the cold, blood vessels to the extremities constrict to reduce heat loss. This leaves the extremities with less blood and therefore colder. This enables the body's core to retain more heat and to stay alive. Life saving as this is, it may leave your extremities frost bitten.

Remember this

Avoid alcohol in the cold as it dilates the blood vessels and allows the release of body warmth. You feel warm as all the heat leaves you but ultimately your body temperature drops.

Muscles and nerves are desensitized and slow to react if cooled. The cold slows you down mentally and physically – you therefore need a plan of action *before* the cold gets too firm a grip, and virtually paralyses you mentally and physically.

The cold also makes us urinate more. This is because blood to the extremities is reduced, so raising the core's blood pressure. The body deals with this increased pressure by offloading some liquid. Dehydration thus becomes a risk. Avoid diuretics like coffee, otherwise you will worsen the situation further.

Anticipation

One of the most important skills, if not the most important skill, of a survivor is the ability to anticipate.

My Suunto Vector wristwatch has a barometer and thermometer, and allows me to see developing weather trends. Several other watches can do the same, and they can easily be bought from a well-stocked outdoor shop or online.

Most of us will be aware of the tremendous cooling effect of the 'wind chill factor'. For example, if the thermometer reads minus 9°C, in a 30 mph wind, your body will react as if it were minus 32°C, and exposed flesh would freeze in around 60 seconds. Be aware of the wind chill factor, and shield yourself against the wind whenever you can, particularly when you stop for a break.

Whether wet from a river crossing or stuck out on the moors in the rain, the body will cool dramatically. Water is 25 times better at conducting heat (away from you) than air. If left unaddressed, hypothermia could follow. Staying dry is of enormous importance even if it is not particularly cold.

Clothing

Adjust your clothing as your body temperature rises and falls. Ideally, have something warm and dry stowed away for when you stop moving, and crawl into your tent or shelter for the night.

Feet: Wear quality socks and consider wearing insulating (or even just shock absorbing) inner soles. To prevent blisters, wear a fine meshed inner sock and then a heavier woollen outer sock on top. To increase the warmth further and to add to the waterproofness, I would also recommend a Gore-Tex sock. These are designed to keep your feet dry in wet conditions, but should also allow water vapour to escape, and not make feet too sweaty. Boots should be fit for the purpose and properly proofed. Tough leather boots are usually up to most conditions and terrains, but many man-made materials are now superb, so have a good look around. In cold and/or wet conditions, gaiters are a must. They keep you warmer and dryer.

Legs: Wear thermal long-johns, like those made by Berghaus, Lowe Alpine or Helly Hansen, as your core layers. Then wear warm but quick-drying trousers; try to avoid wholly cotton stuff as it is pretty hopeless when wet. Waterproof and windproof over-trousers act as your outer protective layer. Breathable fabric is better as you can get very hot if on the move, even in cold, wet conditions.

Trunk: As with your legs, build up several layers starting with a long-sleeve thermal top. The second layer should be a shirt with a collar or polo neck as you need something that protects your neck. Then add a fleece or woollen jumper. Then wear a warm, perhaps down-padded jacket. Note, many companies now produce battery-heated jackets which will produce a low comforting heat for hours at a time before needing recharging. They might be worth considering in some circumstances.

Your outer protective shell should be wind and waterproof, and with a hood. Bright-coloured jackets will be easier for rescuers to find if help is needed. Black and matt green ones may make you dangerously invisible when you want to be anything but.

Head: Much of your body heat is lost through your head and neck. They contain large amounts of hot arterial blood, but are often left uncovered, so heat escapes. You therefore need to cover them and protect against unwanted heat loss in cold conditions.

Remember this

Always carry a scarf and always have some form of head gear with you.
Make sure your hat can't be lost too easily in the wind.

Goggles could be appropriate in snowy or windy conditions,
where damage to the eyes from grit or UV rays is a risk.

Hands: As with socks, wear several pairs. Mittens are warmer
than gloves but it is common practice to wear thinner inner
gloves and thicker waterproof outer mittens. Make sure they
are attached to each other with string up and along your
arms and across your back. If you lose your protection in
extreme conditions, your ability to operate properly becomes
compromised, perhaps with disastrous consequences.

Pocket warmers are handy, but too fiddly and short-lived in my
experience. By all means try one, but don't expect miracles.

Trapped air is a good insulator, which is why old-fashioned
string vests were so effective. In extreme cases you can
improvise by stuffing paper or dry leaves in between layers of
your clothes. This will create a layer of trapped air which will
keep you warm.

'The Eskimo programme'

Eskimos tolerate the cold very well. This is primarily the result
of long-term adaptation. By deliberately under-dressing when
it is not life threatening to do so, you too can become more
accustomed to the cold. Research has shown that intermittent
exposure to the extreme cold causes an increased adaptation
and tolerance of the cold. Leave off that warm jacket next time
you go out, have the odd cold shower, turn the heater off in the
car: freeze a little.

If you always wear warm clothing and work in heated buildings,
your body never gets a chance to acclimatize.

Try it now

Follow a programme of controlled exposure to the cold, so that you begin to feel less cold as the body adjusts. This will help when the unexpected happens and cold conditions are forced upon you. While others become paralysed and clumsy with cold you will find it more bearable and so be able to think and act properly for longer.

Case study

People die from the effects of the cold in very normal conditions, and not just in the pursuit of an adventure sport, mountaineering or polar exploration. In the spring of 2011, in the mid-United States, Rita and Albert Chretien, both in their fifties, came to understand the lethal and deceptive nature of the cold.

They were travelling in their Chevrolet van, from their home in British Columbia to Las Vegas. They were familiar with long journeys, were in good health, and the van was well stocked. They were using the van's GPS to guide them through the network of roads.

While taking a short cut on a remote forestry road their van got stuck in mud. It was not four-wheel drive, and they simply could not free themselves. By now it was getting late, so they decided to spend the night in the van, and covered themselves with spare clothing.

The following day they set about trying to free the van, and appreciated just how remote their location was. It was cold too, with some snow on the ground. They could not get the van free, and spend a very uncomfortable three days in the van, without seeing anyone at all. Albert decided to walk what he believed was about ten miles, to the main highway. He intended getting help and coming back for Rita. He was never seen again.

Meanwhile, Rita unpacked their spare food and clothing, and made herself as warm as she could. It was not a camper van, and they intended eating and sleeping in hotels and motels along the way. Consequently, they had very little food with them. Rita found some trail mix, a few sweets, and some scraps of jerky. She collected water in a plastic container.

Back home in Canada, friends became concerned about the lack of communication, and decided to call the police. The authorities searched for a couple of weeks, and then gave up. They could be anywhere.

Rita kept her spirits up by routinely gathering water, and writing a journal. Days became weeks, and she grew weaker and weaker. Although she carefully rationed out her meagre food, it ran out eventually. Forty-nine days later, having lost around 30 lb Rita had had enough, and prepared to die. Her last diary entry said she was now going to sleep and did not expect to wake up.

But she did wake up, to the sound of noisy hunters on quad bikes; she was found! Rita was airlifted to hospital, and in time, recovered completely from her ordeal. Sadly, her husband Albert was never found, and although presumed dead, his body was never recovered.

Travel

All movement burns calories, which in turn produces heat. The result is that you temporarily feel warmer, but unless you can replace the calories, you will feel very cold when you stop, and your body cools down.

Key idea

The cold reduces the useful life of battery-powered equipment, so bear this in mind if relying upon GPS navigational aids or radio equipment. Navigation in Polar regions is difficult because magnetic compasses become less reliable and very precise calculations are needed; the stars are more accurate.

Skis or snowshoes are usually vital in snowy areas so either bring some or have a contingency plan if travel over snow fields is likely. Moving on foot through deep snow is incredibly fatiguing and will limit what you can carry.

Risks

Frost nip: this is the early stages of frostbite caused by exposure of an extremity (ears, nose, hands, feet) to continued cold. The skin turns white but is not uncomfortable. Treat by covering the affected parts with something soft and warm. Regularly wiggling fingers and toes and pulling funny faces to stretch and exercise your facial muscles will keep blood flowing to the exposed extremities, and so reduce the risk.

Frostbite: the skin turns white and waxy and is now very cold. It is firm to touch and often swollen. The affected parts go numb and may have a blue-ish edge to them. Only if there is no further risk of refreezing should you try thawing out. Treat by soaking in warm water. This will be very painful and blisters are likely to form. Don't pierce them. Do not massage or expose frost-bitten skin to excessive or direct heat. Amputations of black and dead fingers and toes is usually necessary, to prevent poisoning of the blood – which if not done, can result in death.

Trench foot: this is where the feet are exposed to prolonged wet and cold. Blood vessels constrict to reduce heat loss, but unless the foot is dried and warmed, blisters, ulcers and gangrene may occur. Amputation may be required. This common condition can take only 12 hours of exposure to develop and become a serious concern.

Cold burns: this can happen if unprotected flesh, normally hands, touches bare metal in very cold conditions. The flesh 'sticks' to the metal and if pulled away will be left behind. Treat by pouring warm water (urine will do) between the hand and the metal object.

Hypothermia: this is when the body reaches a point where it is unable to warm itself up. Classic symptoms are clumsiness, lethargy, confusion, intense shivering, sudden bursts of energy and irrational behaviour. Treat by trying to dry out wet clothes and getting yourself warm. Eat, and drink hot, sweet drinks if you can.

Hypothermia commonly affects people hiking in cold and wet conditions, who have been walking for hours, and still have hours to go.

If in a group, huddle together when resting or sleeping as your combined body heat will benefit you all. It works for penguins.

Remember this

Death will follow if you ignore or fail to notice the symptoms of hypothermia and do nothing.

Dehydration: the cold makes us urinate more and this, coupled with a tendency to drink less, can induce dehydration. Headaches, nausea, ringing in your ears, irritability and dark urine are all signs. Drink periodically regardless of your thirst.

Teeth: you should note that the cold can loosen fillings slightly and you therefore risk losing them if you eat sticky or chewy sweets. Losing a filling can cause intense pain, and distract you from carrying out a vital task, such as accurate navigation. Even just one bad decision could use up valuable time and resources, and perhaps put you in danger.

Focus points

* A lack of food will expose you to hypothermia and generally feeling cold.
* Check weather forecasts so you are prepared for bad weather ahead, or can remain where you are and perhaps avoid it.
* You lose body heat some 25 times faster if you are wet.
* Wear several layers, not just one or two thick items of clothing.
* The cold reduces the life of batteries, so take spares.
* Do all you can to keep feet dry, as trench foot can start to affect you after only 12 hours.

Next step

This book was meant as a course to be read in order, practising the techniques along the way. By now, you should have slowly built yourself up into someone stronger and more useful to others, and to yourself. What follows is a short test to see how much you have retained, and whether you could survive a few hypothetical situations.

Appendix 1: Survival test

Survival test – 20 questions

Knowledge and skills need to be periodically tested. Tests are a means of checking to see whether we really know what we think we know. Knowledge goes rusty through lack of use, so unless you are in life-threatening situations frequently, survival skills deteriorate through lack of practice. However, too many of us convince ourselves and others that we are as sharp and knowledgeable as ever. The following questions may highlight some weaknesses. Answers are in Appendix 2. Good luck!

THE TEST

1 Survival is often a case of having nothing more than the right frame of mind. List a few of the mental qualities a survivor should have.

2 The right equipment can save your life, but never depend so heavily upon it that its loss spells disaster and renders you useless. Describe some items you would put in a survival kit.

3 Apart from your survival kit, list a few other items of kit that should be carried to help cope with the unexpected.

4 Although dehydration can kill in its own right, it is more often the effects that cause death and disaster beforehand. List some of the early warning signs that should alert you to being dehydrated.

5 Food is fuel. The more calories, the more fuel. How many calories would an average active person need daily, and what types of food are the best sources of energy?

6 Navigational skills prevent you heading into disaster, and can lead you to safety. Imagine you are lost and without your compass. Describe two methods of using the sun to find north.

7 Education and training may be expensive and time consuming, but ignorance is doubly so. Can you recall a few of the uses of ordinary sugar?

8 The cold kills. Hypothermia occurs when your body simply cannot rewarm itself. If you do nothing, you *will* die. What are the early warning indicators?

9 Safety standards are not universally adopted, and rescue facilities vary considerably around the world. Upon boarding a ship for the first time, what are a few preparations you can make to enhance your chances of survival in the event of a disaster at sea?

10 Putting aside actual route planning, list some preparations you should make before heading off on a hike to somewhere unfamiliar.

11 What should your initial course of action be if your vehicle breaks down, or your plane has to make an emergency landing, in either the Arctic or a desert? Assume there are no medical emergencies to worry about.

12 Mosquitoes carry life-threatening diseases and are a persistent irritation in the wild. List a few ways of protecting yourself against them.

13 You have bought yourself a map of a place you have never been to, and are planning a trek through an area of wilderness. What are a few of the factors you should take into account when planning your route?

14 What steps can you take to reduce the risk of dehydration?

15 What are some of the advantages in travelling on a raft down river?

16 Where should you carry a survival kit, and perhaps one or two other useful items of equipment?

17 How would you minimize the risk of being bitten by a snake and/or scorpion?

18 What are your initial considerations when building a shelter?

19 You must always take a medical kit with you into the wilderness, and ensure it is customized to the climate and region you will be in. List some of the medical conditions your medical kit should be prepared to deal with if you are off to a jungle environment.

20 Why might you want to avoid drinking coffee and alcohol in a cold environment?

There is no time limit, but do take the questions seriously. Sadly, there have been too many deaths and serious injuries because people venturing into the outdoors believed things would be alright, and that accidents befall others, not them. They were over confident and over-estimated their knowledge and ability to cope with the unknown. Please do not underestimate the effects of the weather on mountains, in deserts or in the wilderness generally. Similarly, do not underestimate the need to be super self-sufficient in remote regions, as rescue is regrettably not always possible. You need to be your own medic, navigator, cook, survival expert, meteorologist, as well as being a boat and house builder.

Appendix 2: Test answers

Survival test – the answers

How did you do? There is no pass or fail to the test, as not being able to answer just one question correctly could lead to a serious situation, and perhaps death.

If you get a question wrong, your answer was incomplete, or you could not answer at all, you need to refresh your knowledge and skills. Survival skills need to be second nature to anyone who regularly ventures outdoors, perhaps to remote areas and mountains. You need to be able to put survival skills into action without prolonged thought or deliberation, as time may not always be on your side.

THE ANSWERS

1 Common mental attributes of a survivor are an ability to:

  ▷ Think clearly and calmly, and not to panic.

  ▷ Have a positive, optimistic outlook.

  ▷ 'Tune in' and adapt quickly to a new environment.

  ▷ Be assertive and proactive in bringing about positive change.

  ▷ Never give up – a survivor will find energy and drive when others throw the towel in and perhaps die.

2 No one kit is suitable for all situations and occasions. Customize your kit and equipment based upon your knowledge of the terrain, climate and your foreseeable circumstances. Constantly review the items in your kit, and ensure no items are deteriorating. Here is a list of useful items to consider including, but they are only a starting point as to what your kit could contain:

  ▷ flint and striker

  ▷ waterproof matches

- ▷ fishing kit

- ▷ water purification tablets

- ▷ small compass

- ▷ painkillers

- ▷ safety pins

- ▷ 'magic' birthday candles

- ▷ wire saw

- ▷ scalpel blades

- ▷ brass wire

- ▷ heliograph or mirror

- ▷ potassium permanganate

- ▷ needle and thread

- ▷ condom (as a temporary water carrier)

See Chapter 2 for a full list and an explanation of the multi-uses of some items listed.

3 In addition to a small survival kit, other useful kit to take along with you to aid your survival if things do not quite go to plan are:

- ▷ A medical kit, customized to your circumstances and the region/climate you will be in. Medical kits should complement and support your medical knowledge, so make sure this is kept as sharp as your scalpels.

- ▷ A poncho or large plastic sheet. This has many uses, including use as an emergency shelter.

- ▷ Some paracord, or some form of strong cord.

- ▷ Cooking pots or army-style mess tins. A cooking pot is one of the useful items of equipment that is difficult to make in the wilderness, so always take one with you.

- ▷ A strong sheath knife and a smaller multi-tool, e.g. a Swiss army knife or a Leatherman tool.

- ▷ A compass, plus a spare.

▷ A torch, and spare batteries.

▷ A water filter, and water purification tablets.

▷ A fire-lighting kit, e.g. a lighter, sparker, waterproof matches, fire-lighter blocks, cotton wool balls – all in a waterproof container.

▷ A mobile phone or means of emergency communication. Small solar panel chargers and/or spare emergency mobile chargers are now easy to obtain and should also be taken with you.

4 Signs you may be suffering from dehydration include:

▷ dark urine

▷ headaches

▷ irritability

▷ fatigue

▷ nausea

▷ ringing in your ears

▷ confusion

5 An average, active person would need around 3,500 calories per day. This should be doubled in very cold conditions. Fats have the highest caloric value, and examples include nuts, eggs, fish and animal meat. The second food choice you should go for is carbohydrates. Good sources include fruit, roots, tubers, honey, bread, pasta, rice and biscuits.

If you are able to take some emergency food, perhaps inside a cooking pot, these are the foods to pack and stow away.

6 The two main methods of solar (sun) navigation are:

▷ The shadow tip method – put a stick around a metre in length in the ground. Put a stone on the shadow's tip. Wait at least 20 minutes, then put another stone on the shadow's tip again; it will have moved by now. The first stone will indicate west, and the second east. North and south can be found quite easily now.

▷ The wristwatch method – ensure your watch is set to local time, and point the hour hand at the sun. Draw and imaginary line halfway between the 12 and the hour hand. North will be behind you, and at the bottom of your imaginary line, furthest from the sun.

7 Sugar is useful if dehydrated, as sweet drinks are better than plain water when you need to rehydrate yourself. Pouring neat sugar into a wound has been found to accelerate healing, slow down bleeding, and ward off infection. Sugar can also make foul-tasting food (and medicine), palatable. It can boost your blood-sugar if you are depleted and needing short-term energy.

8 Signs of hypothermia include:

▷ clumsiness

▷ lethargy

▷ confusion

▷ intense shivering

▷ sudden burst of energy

▷ irrational behaviour

▷ skin becomes very pale and waxy

9 Surviving a sinking ship can be made easier if, upon boarding the ship, you do the following:

▷ Find where the life-jackets are stowed and try one on. Valuable time will be saved if you do this before disaster strikes and chaos and icy water are all around you.

▷ Walk around the ship and get to know the layout, exits, staircases, location of life rafts, etc. This could be life-saving knowledge if you have to abandon ship, perhaps in the dark, and perhaps in a hurry.

▷ Know the ship's route and the estimated distance from land and any islands it will pass.

▷ Have a waterproof 'grab bag' that can be snatched immediately, and which contains a survival kit customized to sea travel, including some emergency food and water, as well as flares and/or emergency beacons.

10 Before you go anywhere:

▷ Check the weather forecast and usual climate for the time of year you will be there. There is no point heading off during the monsoon or rainy season if you help it. Knowing the likely weather and climate will assist in equipment and clothing selection.

▷ Advise someone of your route and estimated time of arrival at a given point. This is to ensure a rescue attempt is initiated if you go missing, and to guide rescuers to the right area.

▷ Note the time the sun rises and sets, and to avoid you being caught out in an unfamiliar place in the dark.

▷ Refresh and review your medical and survival skills. Customize them to where you are going, and the likely risks of the area.

11 Vehicles and aircraft are easier for rescuers to see than a lone person wandering in the wilderness, probably in clothes of a similar colour to the terrain. Your mode of transport will also offer a form of shelter. Always stay with your vehicle initially. Protect yourself against the weather and any dangerous or unpleasant wildlife, be they insects or wolves. Next, signal for help, or at least have a signal ready to go once you think someone is close by. Finally, assess your equipment, food and water. Make a plan before you are too weak to do anything.

12 You can protect yourself against malaria-carrying mosquitoes by:

▷ Covering up as much as possible. Wear long-sleeved shirts and long trousers. This is especially important at dusk when the females feed.

▷ Pre-soaking or spraying your clothing in insect repellent with a high DEET content.

▷ Using a mosquito head net while working or moving around.

▷ Sleeping under a mosquito net at all times.

▷ Burning a smoky fire once you pitch camp.

▷ Camping in a windy spot.

▷ Taking anti-malaria tablets, the type advised by a specialist in tropical medicine.

13 To ensure you reach your objective safely and on time, take into account the following:

▷ The terrain (e.g. swamps), the contours, and the likely need to cross rivers where there are no bridges.

▷ The estimated, realistic, daily mileage. Have a contingency plan if you fall behind and cannot reach your daily objective due to injury or delay.

▷ Your food and water needs, and the opportunities to refill and resupply on the way.

▷ Suitable places to camp out.

▷ Daylight hours available at the time of year you will be there.

▷ Weather forecast and the usual climate for when you will be there.

▷ Hazards that could prove a problem, e.g. wildlife, insects, monsoons, hurricanes, unsafe water supplies.

14 You can slow down your rate of dehydration by doing all you can to conserve what fluids you have. Take the following precautions:

▷ Eat less, especially fatty foods, as water is needed in the digestion process.

▷ Do not smoke, and refrain from drinking coffee or alcohol – all will make matters worse.

▷ Stop talking and only breathe through your nose. Water, as vapour, is lost every time you open your mouth.

▷ Keep cool by wetting clothes in undrinkable water, e.g. sea-water, even urine.

▷ Reduce physical activity until the coolest parts of the day.

▷ Wear loose clothing and cover exposed skin to reduce water loss through evaporation.

▷ Get out of the sun and the heat if you can, and do not lie or sit on any hot surfaces.

15 Travelling by river raft, especially in a jungle, has many advantages over travelling by foot, where progress may only be a few miles a day. Consider the following:

▷ It enables you to travel faster, particularly in areas where travelling over land will be slow and difficult.

▷ It allows you to travel if weak or injured.

▷ It enables you to carry heavy or cumbersome equipment through difficult terrain.

▷ It enables you to carry wounded companions more comfortably than on a stretcher.

▷ A good raft will keep you dry, and away from potentially dangerous land and river animals.

▷ Travelling down river by raft will require fewer calories per mile than travelling by foot.

16 On you, and at all times, for example in a pouch on your belt, or in a secure trouser pocket. Do not put your survival kit or other vital equipment in your rucksack or jacket pocket. Jackets and rucksacks are always being put down and taken off. The usefulness of a survival kit relies on it *always* being attached to you.

17 You can minimize the chances of being bitten or stung by a snake or scorpion by taking into account the following:

▷ Research the area and know what is there before you get there.

▷ Be cautious of sunny spots in a forest: snakes may be sunning themselves.

▷ Be aware of snakes hanging down from trees and curled around branches.

▷ Snakes and scorpions are often found under rocks and logs.

▷ Most bites are below the knee, so wear adequate boots, gaiters and long trousers.

▷ Stamp your feet or bang the ground with a heavy walking stick as you enter 'snake territory' as this may scare them off; many bites occur because snakes are startled or accidentally trodden on.

▷ Seal any uncooked meats you may have with you, as snakes and other animals are attracted to them.

▷ Sleep off the ground. Insects, scorpions and snakes will bother you less, particularly as some are heat seeking. Shake out all clothes and boots every morning.

18 If building some form of shelter is going to enhance your survival, you must try to build it with calorie/energy conservation in mind, and not work yourself to near death. You may have insufficient food to restock yourself. You should therefore adapt a natural feature, such as a cave or fallen tree, rather than try to build a four-walled log cabin.

19 Your jungle medical kit should be expanded and customized to deal with the following:

▷ dehydration

▷ heatstroke

▷ infected cuts

▷ malaria and fevers generally

▷ insect bites, including spiders and scorpions

▷ snake bites, there are an awful lot of them in jungle areas

▷ other animal bites

▷ stomach upset/diarrhoea

▷ pain

20 Avoid alcohol in the cold as it dilates the blood vessels and allows the release of body heat. You feel warm as all

the heat leaves you, but ultimately your body temperature drops. You should also avoid coffee and other high caffeine drinks as they are diuretics and will make you pass water more frequently. This is both inconvenient in the cold, but may also lead to dehydration – a condition not often thought of as being associated to cold environments. Thirst is an unreliable indicator of your water needs, and in the cold you may not appreciate the need to drink frequently.

Appendix 3: Survival tips

Ten survival tips that could keep you alive

Survival is about having an awareness of your present and future needs, as well as about the environment around you. It's about adaptability and resilience. This section of the book is meant as a reminder, an *aide mémoire*, and not as a substitute to reading the preceding chapters. The ten tips that follow are a summary of key points which will help keep you out of trouble.

1 RESEARCH

Learn as much as possible about the region you are going to beforehand. Find out about the climate, approximate times of sunrise and sunset, as well as the general geography and terrain. Read up on the plants and animals that are likely to be present during the period you will be there.

Obtain accurate maps and note the magnetic variation, if stated, to enable accurate navigation. Try to commit to memory the topography and route you intend taking. Memorize the landmarks, rivers, roads and towns as best you can.

Check with your doctor or someone who specializes in medicine for the region you are heading off to.

Read accounts of what life is like in the region you are going to. Look into every aspect of the area; you never know what tiny scrap of information may prove useful if things go wrong.

2 ANTICIPATE AND PREPARE

Play 'what if?' Invent worst-case scenarios and prepare a course of action to overcome them. For example, what if the river you intend refilling your water containers at is dry? Where is the next nearest source? Or what if you have to spend a night out on the mountain due to injury – do you have an emergency bivvy bag, a means of signalling for help, or even a first aid kit? What if your map becomes lost or damaged? Do you have a spare?

Collect firewood before it is dark; attend to wounds and blisters before they become serious; charge up your mobile phone in anticipation of an emergency; practise erecting your tent in the dark; bring spare torch batteries; heighten your awareness of the effects of dehydration and hypothermia. Think ahead!

Anticipate likely scenarios and set-backs that could realistically befall you. Have a contingency plan that can be put into action if they actually happen. The idea is that by constantly anticipating and preparing for mishaps and needs, you never get into a 'survival situation' in the first place.

3 BE SELF-SUFFICIENT
Rely on no one. Don't expect 'others' to know things for you. On any trip make sure you are capable of being the mechanic, the linguist, the medic, the cook, the navigator, the survival expert, etc. Make sure **you** can look after yourself and get yourself out of trouble. Treat other team members as tools; useful, but not to be relied upon.

4 KEEP ESSENTIAL SKILLS FRESH
Survival skills need to be practised and refreshed regularly, as do your medical skills and knowledge. These are life-saving skills that you cannot afford to neglect and risk going rusty. Do quality courses under expert instruction and attend follow-up refresher courses periodically. Survival and medical skills must become second nature.

Make sure you camp and hike as often as you can, and in all seasons. Become comfortable in conditions others would call adverse. Practise basic skills like fire lighting without matches, finding north without a compass, or making an improvised shelter. Try to gain direct experience of giving medical aid to genuine patients; kill and gut a fish or a rabbit; spend a night outdoors without a tent. Don't risk being too shocked and stunned to be useful in a real-life survival situation.

Read and re-read this book periodically – remind yourself of what you thought you knew.

5 KEEP YOURSELF FIT

Being of superior fitness means you give yourself the edge when the unexpected happens. Sometimes a disaster is averted simply by being able to walk/run to safety, perhaps with an injury, or perhaps when exhausted.

Run, swim, cycle, circuit train. Being fitter and healthier means your body can take more abuse and fend off illness more easily. If you need some guidance on getting fit, join a local gym and ask for a few sessions with a personal trainer and have a programme drawn up. There are a great many books on the subject, some of which are listed in Appendix 4 (Taking things further).

6 CUSTOMIZE YOUR KIT AND CLOTHING

Your survival kit must be packed with knowledge of the foreseeable conditions and circumstances in mind. A fishing kit is usually redundant in the desert, just as water purification tablets are in Polar regions. Customize your survival kit and equipment for each trip.

It sounds obvious, but dress appropriately and check weather forecasts in advance. Boots and jackets may need to be varied depending on the terrain and your circumstances. Review what you intend taking, as there is rarely a piece of clothing or kit that suits all terrains and all regions.

Tailor your medical kit to known and foreseeable risks – don't just pack it full of plasters and aspirin. Based upon your research, you may need specific medicines for your trip. Know how to use the contents without having to refer to manufacturer's details.

Use good-quality equipment and check it regularly for signs of any deterioration. For example, wire-saws rust and medicine have shelf-lives. Your life may depend upon your thoroughness.

7 KEEP ESSENTIAL KIT ON YOU AT ALL TIMES

Survival kits and other vital equipment must be on your person all the time: in your pockets; on your belt; around your neck; sewn into your clothing. **Never** put essential kit in the bottom of your rucksack or in a vehicle. In true emergencies you may have to abandon your luggage and jump or run to safety. Equally, theft or disaster could separate you from your pack and leave you with nothing but the clothes you stand up in.

Be able to survive if your main pack is lost by making sure your remaining clothing houses enough survival equipment to keep you going. Wear a compass watch, carry essential medical kit in a waistband pouch. Wear a Leatherman multi-tool and a survival kit on your belt, and replace your boot laces with paracord. Become a walking survival kit and give yourself the advantage.

8 HAVE A PLAN OF ACTION BEFORE YOU ARE INCAPACITATED

Once you have acknowledged that you are in a potentially life-threatening situation, start planning your escape from it immediately. Act quickly, but don't panic. The effects of adverse weather (hot or cold), as well as food and water deprivation, will inhibit your ability to think clearly. The longer you wait for 'something' to happen, or 'someone' to tell you what to do, the more fatigued and helpless you become. Be proactive and have a plan of action early on. Set up a means of signalling and try to contact rescuers as soon as possible.

If drinking water is going to become an issue, start looking for and collecting it **before** supplies run low and while you still have the energy and ability to do so. Similarly, lay out snares, fishing lines and bird traps as soon as possible **before** food has run out. It is important to stress that you must put several methods of procurement into effect simultaneously. You cannot afford to try one method at a time, moving on only when it proves unsuccessful. Put into effect three or more methods of water procurement. Lay traps, snares and fishing lines while you go off gathering edible plants. Do everything at once to maximize your chances of getting what you need. Time and resources may not allow you the luxury of doing only one at a time.

Don't wait until all your reserves have gone and you are too weak to save yourself.

9 BE CREATIVE AND ABLE TO IMPROVISE

Never rely so heavily on your kit that you could not survive without it. Treat kit as useful, but have the ability to improvise and get by if it becomes lost or damaged. Spoons and tent pegs can easily be fashioned from sticks; ponchos can double up as tents; socks can be used as water filters. Food can be eaten with improvised chopsticks, grass and ferns make comfortable mattresses.

The magnet in a radio speaker can be removed to magnetize a needle and so be used to find north. Paracord can be stripped down and used as fishing line. Never accept equipment failure, as failure. **Expect** losses and damage and think nothing of constructing make-shift equipment and tools. Anyone can survive given all the appropriate kit; you must learn to survive with nothing but your knowledge, resourcefulness and determination.

10 HAVE A POSITIVE MENTAL OUTLOOK

You must be proactive in trying to resolve the difficulties set before you. Don't wait for instructions or guidance on what to do from a 'leader' – lead yourself and take your fate into your own hands.

Adapt and tune in to your new environment. Expect a degree of hardship but don't accept death as an option. **You** have to take the initiative and bring about the required changes. Where there's a will, there's a way.

Negativity breeds failure and to give up hope puts you on the downward spiral and will not allow energy reserves to be drawn upon.

Don't be another victim. While others may lie down to die, you must be able to rise up out of the wreckage, debris or disaster, and walk to safety. Cultivate an inner strength and maintain a clear and focused vision of survival. The survival stories in this book will hopefully show that, although the odds of survival can often be slim, they are never zero.

Appendix 4:
Taking things further

SURVIVAL COURSES

Ray Mears' Woodlore – 01580 819668 / www.raymears.com

Hands On Bushcraft – 07598 491989 / www.handsonbushcraft.co.uk

True Ways Survival – 0800 0430832 / www.truewayssurvival.com

Bear Grylls' Survival Academy – 01483 424438 / www.beargryllssurvivalacademy.com

Barking Mad Survival School – 01480 384426 / www.barkingmadsurvival.co.uk

Survival School – 01453 752220 / www.survivalschool.co.uk

MEDICAL COURSES

Training Expertise – 01256 886543 / www.training-expertise.co.uk

Red Cross – 0844 4122804 / www.redcross.org.uk

Wilderness Medical Training – 01539 823183 / www.wildernessmedicaltraining.co.uk

Prometheus Medical – 01568 613942 / www.prometheusmedical.co.uk

Expedition & Wilderness Medicine – 01234 766778 / www.expeditionmedicine.co.uk

OUTDOOR PURSUIT COURSES

Outward Bound – 01931 740000 / www.outwardbound.org.uk

Plas Y Brenin – 01690 720214 / www.pyb.co.uk

Action Outdoors – 0203 3285443 / www.action-outdoors.co.uk

YHA – 0800 0191700 / www.yha.org.uk

Snow Goose Mountain Centre – 01397 772467 /
www.highland-mountain-guides.co.uk

BOOKS

Some specialist books are only printed in limited supply by the
publishers, so you may have to obtain them either secondhand
or via specialist suppliers such as Paladin Press (www.paladin-
press.com). The title and author alone will enable you to trace
a copy.

Life at the Extremes by Frances Ashcroft

Animal Tracks and Signs by Preben Bang and Preben Dahlstrom

Ultimate Navigation Manual by Lyle Brotherton

The Complete Guide to Tracking by Bob Carss

Mountain and Arctic Survival by Barry Davies

Pocket First Aid and Wilderness Medicine by Dr Jim Duff and
Dr Peter Gormly

The Third Man Factor by John Geiger

Deep Survival by Laurence Gonzales

The Natural Navigator by Tristan Gooley

Medicinal Plants of Britain and Europe by Wolfgang Hensel

Oxford Handbook on Expedition and Wilderness Medicine by
Chris Johnson and others

Extreme Survival by Dr Kenneth Kamler

Survival Psychology by John Leach

Food for Free by Richard Mabey

Build the Perfect Survival Kit by John D McCann

Wild Food by Ray Mears

Stay Alive in the Desert by K E M Melville

The Unthinkable by Amanda Ripley

The Survivors Club by Ben Sherwood

Weather for Hillwalkers and Climbers by Malcolm Thomas

Navigation for Walkers by Julian Tippett

Medicine for Mountaineering and Other Wilderness Activities edited by James A Wilkerson

MAP SUPPLIERS

Stanfords – 0207 836 1321 / www.stanfords.co.uk

Maps Worldwide – 0845 1220 559 / www.mapsworldwide.com

Emap Site – 0118 9736883 / www.emapsite.com

Ordnance Survey – 0845 4560420 / www.ordnancesurveyleisure.co.uk

The Map Shop – 01684 593146 / www.themapshop.co.uk

CLOTHING AND EQUIPMENT SUPPLIERS

Silvermans – 02077 900900 / www.silvermans.co.uk

Nomad Travel – 0845 2600044 / www.nomadtravel.co.uk

Field and Trek – www.fieldandtrek.com

Cotswold Outdoor – 0844 5577755 / www.cotswoldoutdoor.com

Rohan – 0800 8401411 / www.rohan.co.uk

Life Systems – 0118 9811433 / www.lifesystems.co.uk

Survival Aids – 01892 610181 / survivalaids.com

Cool Antarctica – www.coolantarctica.com

BCB International – 02920 433700 / www.bcbin.com

USEFUL ORGANIZATIONS

Expedition Advisory Centre, within the Royal Geographical Society: 0207 5913000 / www.rgs.org. Explorers and travellers have benefited from this organization since 1830.

153 Club: www.the153club.org – dedicated to Saharan travel and exploration.

Explorers Club: www.explorers.org – a long-established American explorers' society, which also has a British branch 01394 450391 / www.britishexplorers.org

Alpine Club: 0207613 0755 / www.alpine-club.org.uk – the world's first mountaineering club and a superb source of information.

MASTA: www.masta-travel-health.com – provides customized medical briefs and a wealth of medical information for travellers off to remote places.

Nomad Travel Clinic: 0845 2600044 / www.nomadtravel.co.uk – can provide medical equipment as well as specific vaccinations and medication for foreign travellers.

MAGAZINES ON SURVIVAL AND OUTDOOR PURSUITS

Magazines that are of interest include: *Bushcraft and Survival Skills*, *Combat and Survival*, *Geographical*, *Trail*, *TGO*, *Mountaineer*, *Canoe and Kayak*, *High*, *Survival Quarterly* and *Complete Survivalist*.

Many of these magazines have an online version and a phone app edition for easy access.

Index